God Bless You,
Betty North

I Am With You

BETTY NORTH

BALBOA.
PRESS
A DIVISION OF HAY HOUSE

All Scripture quotations are taken from the King James Version of the Bible.

Balboa Press books may be ordered through booksellers or by contacting:

Balboa Press
A Division of Hay House
1663 Liberty Drive
Bloomington, IN 47403
www.balboapress.com
1 (877) 407-4847

Print information available on the last page.

ISBN: 978-1-5043-5279-6 (sc)
ISBN: 978-1-5043-5281-9 (hc)
ISBN: 978-1-5043-5280-2 (e)

Library of Congress Control Number: 2016904202

Balboa Press rev. date: 04/20/2016

I wish to thank my son Robert. He has been a great help and an encouragement to me.

I died two times, but each time Jesus sent me back to be a witness. He told me he wanted more gold nuggets.

Contents

Preface

In 1944, I, at the age of sixteen, became a child of God. I had a very strong desire to know the Lord. The first thing I did was that I bought myself a new Bible and started to read it, beginning at the first page. I took that Bible with me everywhere I went. Every time I came to a command or a verse that was instructing me on how to live, I underlined it, as it was a special verse to me. I wanted to have a close walk with my Lord. The year 1944 was the start of the great love that developed between the Lord and me.

For a long time I had been praying that the Lord would use me in a special way. I was very blessed by the Lord. The start of my journey was marked by a vision of the Lord I had in 1948.

When I was very young, a pastor told me that I should keep a journal of everything that happened to me. Over a period of time, some of the events might dim, he told me, and I would need to read about them if I wanted to remember them well. This journal would keep every dream or vision clear in my mind.

I have received much encouragement to put together a book. Here I have compiled from my journals several dreams, visions, and miracles that have had a big effect on my life. I believe these experiences will be a help to others. All of these dreams, visions, and miracles drew me closer to the Lord. My faith and trust in Him grew as a result.

It is my desire that others may experience a loving relationship with the Lord as I.

Introduction

I am a retired great-grandmother, eighty-seven years of age. I came to know the Lord very early on, during my young years. When I was a child, I went to church, where I had the honor of sitting in one of the little green wooden chairs specially made to fit a small child.

In 1944 I accepted the Lord as my Savior. At that time, I had graduated from high school and was ready to go out to conquer the world. I had many things in mind that I wanted to do with my life. I had received my pilot's license at sixteen. I was going to work for an accountant.

The most important thing about that year was having the Lord in my life. Jesus, not me, is what this book is about. Throughout my life, Jesus has done many special things for me and my family. I want you to know that Jesus can be very special to you too. Many people have encouraged me to write a book in order to record the things that have happened to me that have involved the Lord. I had no intention of writing a book. I had written about each occurrence that took place using a special notebook that served as my diary. It was like having a huge diary about Jesus. From that diary I selected a few of the dreams, visions, and miracles. I present those here, within these pages, in chronological order.

You will find that I do not use many names in this book. Most of the people I refer to have gone on to be with the Lord. Many have moved all over this great country; I have no Idea where they might be living.

It has been a real blessing to me to be able to reread my diary and reflect on the many things the Lord has done for me. It has drawn me closer to the Lord. When working on this book, I found myself laughing and crying at the greatness of my God and at all he has done.

God gave his perfect Son, Jesus, to be crucified in order to atone for every person's sins. Jesus loves us very much. He consented to be crucified so that every person could have the choice to accept him as Savior or not. The Lord desires to have a personal relationship with you. He wants to make a difference in your world.

I pray that as you read this book you will learn from my experiences with the Lord.

There is one thing I hope you never forget: God is always with you. He does not answer everyone in the same way. Every person is special to him. He understands your every need, and His love for you surpasses all understanding.

My reason for writing this book is to share what God has done for me and what he will do for you.

I give thanks to God for the miracles. I give thanks to God for the things he does for me every day, some of which I take for granted. I give thanks for all the things God is going to do, as he is not finished with me yet. I pray that I will live my life with God always ahead of me. I never want to get ahead of him and get in his way.

Vision of Christ

Summer 1948

I became a Christian at the age of sixteen in 1944 During the two years that followed, I tried to absorb everything I could about my Lord. Before I had the vision I am about to describe, there were many things I did not understand when I read the Bible. The more I read and studied about my Jesus, the more I wanted to learn about him and his great love for us. He was my Lord; I wanted a close walk with him.

I spent my life reading the Bible and trying to retain as much as I could about Jesus. I was changing, but the change was not sudden. Very slowly the Lord changed my whole outlook on life.

Two years flew by. School was behind me. I was young, an eighteen-year-old woman who thought that the whole world revolved around her. I had been working for the Indiana Bell Telephone Company as a telephone operator, and I hosted a radio show on Mondays, Wednesdays, and Fridays at 6:00 p.m. I had to

1

practice a lot before each show. It was not just a talk show; I also played the marimba for the listening audience.

A Mountaintop Experience

I became a new Christian. I was baptized and received Jesus Christ as my Savior. I received a joy and a peace I had never known before.

Then one night, I knelt by my bed and prayed to the Lord about a serious matter. I was being pursued by someone who was obsessed with the idea that I should marry him. The stalking and alarming messages filled my heart with fear. I was scared, and Jesus knew it. I don't remember the words of the prayer now, but I do remember that I had gone to the only One who could help me: Jesus.

After rising from a kneeling position, I turned and sat on the edge of my bed. I pulled my feet up and started to pull the covers over me when I saw Jesus standing there. He was right beside the bed. He was beautiful. He was perfect. I could not say anything. I could not take my eyes off of my Lord Jesus.

I felt a great love radiating from him. There was a great peace that flooded the room. His presence left me awestruck. His hair was between a golden blond color and a light, soft brown. I cannot describe it. I had never seen such beautiful hair. His hair and beard blended together perfectly—not one hair was out of place. He was so perfect, I couldn't move.

Jesus's skin was a beautiful tan. His face showed great strength and power, yet it radiated love, gentleness, and compassion. Jesus had a strong, firm, and reassuring voice. He spoke with love and authority. The way he spoke to me showed his grace toward me and the great concern he had for me. Jesus was here.

I just sat there absorbing what I was seeing and feeling. A lot of people later asked me to describe what Jesus looked like. The best I can tell you is that he is the most handsome man I have ever seen.

Jesus was very tall and was dressed in a long white flowing robe. He had a long cord-like belt that gathered his robe around his waist loosely. I sat in amazement, absorbing my Jesus, who was standing close to me.

Jesus's first words to me were, "How are you?"

I replied, "I'm fine."

He stated with a firm voice of rebuke, "No, you're not." Then he said with concern and love, "Whatsoever you ask in my name, believing, you will receive it." Jesus turned slightly and took a step toward the foot of the bed. He turned again and looked at me. I felt the deep concern he had for me. He stated with a positive firmness, "You have been very worried."

I said, "Yes, I have been."

He knew all about me and what was going on without my telling him—and I knew what he was talking about. He said, "You needn't worry anymore. I have taken care of the matter for you." Again Jesus said, "Whatever you ask in my name, I will do it."

Jesus moved slowly to the foot of my bed, which had a high, solid footboard across the end. He turned and placed his hands on the footboard, again looking directly into my eyes. He knew my every thought and feeling. He stated, "You are very worried about your father."

I answered, "Yes, I am."

Jesus informed me, "I'm going to speak to your father right now." Then he said to me for the third time, "Whatever you ask in my name, I will do it." He just stood there with his hands upon the footboard and looked at me. Then he said in a loving voice, "The matter you have been so troubled about has already been taken care of."

Jesus turned, walked through the bedroom door, and went to the center of the living room. He turned and walked into the kitchen. I could see him no more, but I heard the kitchen door open and then close again. I knew he was going into the shop to see my father.

I leaned as far over in my bed as I possibly could to look out my window. The window overlooked the backyard. I knew Jesus had gone through the door and would be walking across the backyard to the shop, where the garage was.

I waited for Jesus to come into view. He passed the huge apple tree and walked up two steps to ground level. He was beautiful. His white robe revealed his sandals at every stride. He walked so smoothly that it was as though he was gliding across the yard. Once he reached the garage door, he took hold of the doorknob. After opening the door, he stepped into the shop and then closed the door behind him.

I have no knowledge of what happened next. I had been up on my arms and twisted sideways, looking out my bedroom window to see Jesus every second I possibly could. When I awoke in the morning, I realized I had not yet lain down. I was lying on my side across the bed. The night had slipped by. I've always wondered if Jesus had my guardian angel lay me down. Jesus gave me such peace, a peace surpassing all understanding, that I had fallen into a deep sleep that no human being would be able to describe. I certainly cannot explain what had happened to me. I have not had a deep sleep like that since.

What Happened Next

My father was always up before anyone else in the house arose. The morning after Jesus visited me, I heard the back door open. My father came in from the shop. He said to me, "Betty, I have decided to go to church with you. I want to be saved and baptized." He had determination in his voice. He had made up his mind about what he was going to do. He said he had seen a very big change in me and that he wanted the same thing to happen in his life.

This came as no big surprise to me, since I had seen Jesus go into the shop to talk with my father. As mentioned, I don't know what went on in the shop. My father did not see or talk to Jesus as I did, but the following week my father went to church, accepted Christ as his Savior, and was baptized.

You may be wondering what happened with regard to my panicking about the young man who kept calling me. I now had a great peace about that situation. The phone stopped ringing its usual ten to fifteen times a day. I received not one more phone call. No one was waiting for me after work. No messages were sent to me through other people. There was no more fear or worry. The problem had completely vanished as though it had never existed. Jesus had taken it all away.

Overjoyed

My mind was set on seeing and talking with Jesus. He captivated my mind. All I could see or talk about was Jesus. I was so excited about what had happened to me that I just had to share it—or else I would explode. What happened next was not what I had been expecting. Apparently I still had much to learn.

Sharing My Experience

Two of my friends had come to visit me and my family. I just had to tell them about my vision.

They seemed interested in the story as I shared what I'd seen. But I could tell by the looks on their faces that they did not believe it was real. "Oh, you just had a dream," they said. I felt let down. Their ridicule of my supernatural experience with the Lord was disheartening. Then I realized that their knowledge of the scriptures was severely limited to special holiday church services, such as Christmas and Easter. I learned a hard lesson about sharing precious moments with unbelieving friends. Sometimes we don't know our friends as well as we think we do. I wished I had not shared my precious vision with them. They did not understand it at all.

Then one afternoon there was a gathering of churchwomen at our house. One by one they shared with one another. There were a number of things shared. When it came to be my turn, they asked, "Do you have anything to say? You generally have a funny story to tell." I decided that this was an opportunity for me to tell them about my vision. These were churchgoing women, so they would understand what I was talking about.

After I had shared my vision with these women, I got another shock. The only comment I got was, "That's nice. You really had a good dream, didn't you?" They changed the subject, all of them moving on to talk about something else. They knew nothing about dreams or visions. Again, I wished I had not shared my vision with them. I then felt a great need to share it with someone who would understand.

In my quest to share this beautiful thing that had happened to me with someone who would know what I was talking about, I decided to speak with my pastor. I called him to find out if he was home. Once I learned that he was home, I asked if I could come to see him. He told me to come right over, saying that he was sitting on his front porch and enjoying the beautiful day. I walked several blocks to get to the pastor's home. He welcomed me with the same big warm smile he always had.

After some chitchat about family, work, and the weather, we got down to the serious matter at hand. I excitedly told him about my vision, recounting it in just the way it had happened. When I finished, he looked at me with a frown on his face. He was no longer smiling. His reply was, "There have been many faithful, devout ministers and people of God who have spent many hours in prayer asking to have a vision of Jesus. Maybe you were thinking about Jesus and as a result just had a nice dream. You have been saved for such a short time and really know little about the Bible." He tried to say all of this in a nice way.

It did not come across as very nice to me, however. To me, the sound of his voice was like a reprimand. The way he had spoken his words, and the tone of his voice, was stern. What came through to me was this: "Young lady, who do you think you are? Big men of God have not seen Jesus, although they deserve to. You have just been saved and don't know anything yet."

I was shocked by the pastor's reply. I thanked him for his time and then headed for home. Tears welled up in my eyes. I cried on the way home. The one special person I had shared my experience with, the person whom I thought would understand, didn't think it was possible for me to have such a great thing happen. But Jesus had been there in my room. He had talked with me just as I would talk to anyone else. It was no dream. It was a vision that I had taken part in. It was real. I wanted to shout it from the housetops.

I didn't share my vision of Jesus with anyone else for a long time after that. I felt it had to remain a secret between the Lord and me. I hid it in my heart. I felt like Jesus and I had the biggest secret in the world. I knew Jesus loved me so much that he had come to me in a vision. I had lived the experience with him. I know what he told me to do. He said to ask, believe, and receive.

Many weeks later when I was reading the Bible, I came across the three verses that Jesus had said to me. He had quoted them right from the Bible. I was very excited when I found them. I shared all of these verses with my family. I decided that if Jesus wanted me to share my vision of him with someone, then he was going to have to tell me to do so.

As a result, I asked Jesus to tell me when he wanted me to share this vision with someone. And I have shared it with many people over the years. Now, after all these years, I am sharing it with you. *Ask, believe, and receive.*

My Special Verses

John 15:7: "If ye abide in me, and my words abide in you, ye shall ask what ye will, and it shall be done unto you."

John 15:16: "That whatsoever ye shall ask of the Father in my name, he may give it you."

John 16:23: "Whatsoever ye shall ask the Father in my name, he will give it you."

More Verses

John 16:24: "Hitherto have ye asked nothing in my name: ask and ye shall receive, that your joy may be full."

John 16:26: "At that day ye shall ask in my name: and I say not unto you, that I will pray the Father for you."

Matthew 7:7–8: "Ask, and it shall be given you; seek, and ye shall find; knock, and it shall be opened unto you: For every one that asketh receiveth; and he that seeketh findeth; and to him that knocketh it shall be opened."

Matthew 21:22: "And all things, whatsoever ye shall ask in prayer, believing, ye shall receive."

Matthew 6:8: "For your father knoweth what things ye have need of, before ye ask him."

John 14:13–14: "And whatsoever ye shall ask in my name, that will I do, that the Father may be glorified in the Son. If ye shall ask any thing in my name, I will do it."

An Issue of Blood

August 1957

> And, behold, a woman, which was deceased with an issue of blood twelve years, came behind Him, and touched the hem of his garment: For she said within herself, if I may but touch his garment, I shall be whole. But Jesus turned him about, and when he saw her, he said, Daughter, be of good comfort, thy faith hath made thee whole. And the woman was made whole from that hour.
>
> Matthew 9:20–22

There were two distinct differences between me and the woman mentioned in Matthew 9:20–22. My sickness was not for a period of twelve years, and I had not lived in the period when Jesus was in the flesh and walked on earth. I could not reach out and physically touch the garment he was wearing. I thank God that he left a provision for us to reach out and touch Jesus by faith.

I had just gone to the doctor again. Indeed, I had been going to the doctor for quite some time. I do not recall the exact length of time that I was sick, but I was suffering from something that slowly had gotten worse over a period of several years. This last visit was different, though. This time, my doctor said, "There is nothing more I can do for you. I have tried everything that I know to help you. There are doctors experimenting with a new surgery at Mayo Clinic. It has not been perfected yet."

The doctor then asked, "Who came with you?"

I replied, "I drove myself. No one came with me."

The doctor wanted to drive me back to the drive-in restaurant that my husband and I owned. He flatly stated that I could not drive back alone. He had an office full of patients at the time. I assured him that I would be perfectly fine driving myself. He said that his receptionist would drive me, but I declined his offer. I just needed to be alone. He let me go after I agreed to call him as soon as I reached my destination.

I climbed in behind the steering wheel of the station wagon. The full force of what the doctor had said had just begun to sink in. Those were shocking words to have heard. I did not know the full ramifications of what he had said. There was no cure for me. There was no surgery that would correct my problem. I started crying, and I ended up crying all the way back to the drive-in. There were two times when I was crying so hard that I pulled off the road.

I pulled in behind the drive-in and just sat there. My three sons, Bob Jr. (seven years old), Kerry (four years old), and Garry (one year old), came out. They began laughing and playing alongside the station wagon. They were all wanting to tell me about something at the same time. I watched them more closely than I had ever watched them before. When I knew I was facing death, I suddenly realized that my children were the most important people on this earth. The reality had hit. Frantic thoughts were running through my mind: *What will happen to them? Who will be raising my three sons?*

It was at this point that I looked up to heaven and said, "God, if this is your will for me, I want only your will. But, God, I would like to raise my three sons."

The things that happened from then on were planned by God.

I was getting much worse. I was very weak, so weak, in fact, that I could not even make the trip home that night. We lived on a farm that was a thirty-mile drive from Marion, Indiana. I and my family stayed in Marion that night.

My husband and I had built a garage and converted it into a playroom for the boys. It had two hide-a-beds that the boys could sleep on whenever they were with us. I could not travel home because of my severe weakness. I had never been that weak before. And yet I knew that God's hand was working on my behalf.

At 4:00 a.m., there came a knock at the door. Bob, my husband, hurriedly answered the door. It was very unusual for someone to bang on the door this early in the morning. When Bob opened the door, he found his brother standing there. Bob's brother, a minister, had been staying at the church campgrounds in Fairmount for an annual convention. He asked, "Is Betty here? Is she sick?" I heard Bob tell him I was very sick.

Bob's brother then related what had happened to him. He said that he and his wife were staying in one of the cottages at the campgrounds. They had been attending the convention, which had started that week. In the night, he all of a sudden came out of a sound sleep and was wide awake. He heard God speak to him: "Go get Betty. Bring her to the healing service this morning."

He got out of bed and started getting dressed. His wife awoke and asked, "What in the world are you doing getting dressed in the middle of the night?" He proceeded to tell her that God had wakened him to tell him to go get me and bring me to the healing service. He said, "I am on my way to get Betty."

This is a miracle that was part of a series of things that God was working out in my life. Thank God for Bob's brother's obedience. God's divine hand was now with Bob's brother, Harold. Harold thought that he was going to be driving the thirty miles to the farm to get us, as this was where he had expected us to be. As he came near to Marion, he intended to turn onto Thirty-Eighth Street and go past the Veterans Hospital. He thought that would be the shortest way to go, but he missed the turn. God had him miss that turn. As Harold was driving down the bypass, he spotted our station wagon at the drive-in. He knew we were there.

He relayed to us that there was a healing service that morning at 6:00. In his excitement, he told us how God had wakened him and spoken very clearly to him. He was to come and take me to the healing service. He asked me, "Will you come with me to the healing service?"

It did not take any of us very long to get ourselves ready to go. As we finished getting ready, I heard voices singing a beautiful song of praise. I thought, *I know God loves me. He's going to heal me at the special healing service.* God had sent for me. God had a plan for my life, and I did not want to be late. He wanted me to raise my three sons.

* * *

We all sat in a huge tabernacle building on hard wooden seats in the dampness and chill of the early morning. I could hardly wait for the meeting to start.

I was having my normal backache and pain, which had become a large part of my life by this time. It was getting greater and greater every day. All of this pain was making me weaker by the day, too. The chill and the dampness magnified the pain. I didn't care this morning. I was in wonder about what God was going to do.

Slowly, people began to come into the tabernacle. I knew my miracle was about to happen. The minister talked about healing. We prayed. The time that I had been anticipating finally came. Those who wanted healing were to come forward and kneel at the altar. My heart was pounding in anticipation of what was going to happen. I was shaking a little, and I was very weak in the knees. I got up quickly and knelt at a long altar with a wooden rail. The altar was full of people who needed healing.

Several of the ministers were standing together and talking at the other end of the altar. I felt panic starting to set in. Could I last that long if they started clear down there? There were two elderly gentlemen to the right of me. I think I prayed softly to myself. As I was praying, I looked up and saw that the group of ministers had split up. Four of them were coming toward my end.

They talked with the first man and then started praying for him. I prayed for this man as they were praying for him. They talked with the second man, and I prayed for him while they were praying. I remember praying for each one of the people as the pastors prayed for their healing. The ministers spent a little time with the second man, making sure they had prayed for everything he needed.

The four ministers moved over and came to stand in front of me. I thought they would ask me questions and talk to me like they had done with the first two men. One of the men said something to the rest of them, and then all four men laid their hands on my head and started praying. I began to feel a very hot burning sensation in my big toes. Then, starting like electricity from my big toes, it began slowly to work its way up through my legs and into my body. My body was trembling as the sensation started moving down both arms toward my fingertips. This electric feeling went up through my neck. When it reached my head, I heard Pastor Wiley yell, "Do you feel that? This woman got her healing. Did you feel that?" All the pastors were talking together about what each one of them had felt. They were all praising God and thanking him, because there was no doubt with any of them that I was completely healed. They knew I had received a miracle. I was healed. God had allowed them to feel his healing power.

I was still in awe about all that had happened to me. I was not able to say anything for a while. But inside I was thanking and praising God. This was God's miracle for me. I knew I was healed. God had completely healed me. Every man who had laid hands on me had felt the heat and the electricity that I had felt.

Now, when I watched my three sons at play or after they had gone to bed at night, I remembered the short prayer I had prayed after the doctor told me there was nothing more he could do for me. At such a time of hopelessness is when God steps in. This is when he lets you know that when there is nothing more that human beings can do, there is something that he *can do*.

Matthew 19:26: "With men this is impossible, but with God all things are possible."

Luke 1:37: "For with God nothing shall be impossible."

Garry's Eyes

I had a grease fire in the kitchen. Garry, who was eight years old at the time, had both of his eyes splattered by the flaming grease. Bob and I raced him to the hospital, where an eye specialist was waiting for us to arrive. (We had called ahead.)

The staff took Garry into the emergency room immediately. I looked for somewhere to pray. There was no available prayer room, so I made my own. Kneeling on the floor at the foot of an empty wheelchair, I prayed. I don't remember for how long I prayed, but I do recall that I prayed for God to spare Garry's eyes.

The doctor came out and told Bob and me that there was very little hope that Garry would ever see again. His eyes had been burned very badly. The doctor gave us no hope that Garry would ever see again. He stated that he had done everything that was within his power to do. The staff were now taking Garry up to the floor where he would be staying.

It was soon found that there were no available rooms at this time, so they put Garry along a wall in a hallway. I had a chair at the head of his bed. I prayed and prayed. For hours I must have said, "God, heal Garry's eyes."

Only one family member was allowed to stay with Garry. I would not leave, so Bob went home after saying that he had some very important things he needed to do. Later, he told me he had called every pastor he knew. He wanted people praying for Garry. He called his brother in California who was at a pastors' convention. Bob asked his brother to pray for Garry, and then his brother presented the prayer request to the other pastors. We had many people praying for our son, knowing that our God answers prayers.

Very late in the evening, around ten o'clock, I had a peace come over me like I had never felt before. It flooded my very being. I was wrapped in a warmth that I knew was supernatural. How long I felt it, I do not know. But I knew one thing: God was telling me not to worry, that Garry's' eyes were going to be all right. My son was healed.

I started praising the Lord for healing Garry's eyes. I knew that it was done.

Bob came flying down the hall sometime after midnight. He raced up to me and said, "Garry's eyes are going to be all right. God told me that Garry's eyes are going to be okay. I just had to come up and tell you. He's going to see."

We both cried. Then I relayed to Bob what had happened to me while I was praying. The very same time I had been praying, Bob had been praying at home. He said he had been pacing back and forth, and walking around and around the swimming pool in the backyard, when a peace that he had never known before flooded him. We recalled at what time each of us had felt this peace and ultimately found that both of us had been enveloped in God's peace at about the same time.

The next morning, the hospital staff moved Garry into a room. The doctor came to check him and again relayed to me his opinion that Garry would not see, saying that I had better prepare myself for a different kind of life, one with an eight-year-old son who could not see. The doctor, informing me that Garry's bandages would be taken off in three days, said that he would know the extent of the burns at that time. He expected much scarring.

I told the doctor that I knew Garry's eyes were going to be all right. He thought I was nuts. He told Bob that Bob should prepare me for the inevitable. The doctor then called the pastor of the church I and my family attended. He flatly stated to the pastor there that I was not accepting the reality that Garry's eyes had been burned. The doctor asked my pastor to come to the hospital and try to talk sense to me.

That afternoon, the pastor and the assistant pastor came to see my son Garry and to talk to me. They talked with Garry for a while, and then they called me into the hall for our talk. My pastor told me what the doctor had told him about Garry's eyes. I proceeded to tell him what had happened to me and to Bob. I told him and the assistant pastor about God's peace flooding our very being. I said that both Bob and I knew that Garry's eyes were healed.

As the two men were leaving, I could see them shaking their heads. To them I was not accepting reality. But I knew what I knew. No one was going to shake my belief.

It was a long wait for that third day to come. I continued to praise the Lord. I kept thanking the lord for Garry's healing.

The doctor came in about midmorning on that third day. He had brought with him the new young doctor whom he had handpicked to go into practice with him. The first doctor, very businesslike, wanted this new doctor to see Garry's eyes. The doctors pulled the blinds down and turned out the lights. The room became quite dark.

The first doctor talked with Garry, explaining what he was going to do. He was going to shine a light into his eyes to take a good look at them. Once he did so, he asked Garry if he could see the light. Garry answered, "Yes." The two doctors exchanged some very softly spoken comments that I could not hear. The first doctor turned and gave me a very peculiar look. He proceeded to check Garry's eyes and then asked that the blind be raised two or three inches.

The light that came into the room from that small opening was quite bright. Garry was asked if he could see the light. He replied, "Yes, at the bottom of the window."

"Does it hurt your eyes?" the primary doctor asked.

Garry's quick reply was, "No. My eyes don't hurt."

I kept saying over and over, "Thank you, Jesus. Thank you for healing Garry's eyes."

The doctors went on to check more and to raise the blind a little higher. One asked, "What do you see?"

Then the other asked Garry, "Does it hurt your eyes to look at the light?" He held up his fingers and asked, "How many do you see?"

As the doctors kept this up, asking their questions, the first doctor turned, looked at me with a very puzzled expression, and asked, "How did you know?"

The younger doctor stated flatly to his partner, "You had me leave my office full of patients to come over here and see a boy who has severe burns to his eyes? There is not one thing wrong with this boy's eyes."

The doctor said, "I have it all written down on his chart. Look at it. Emergency will verify it. This boy's eyes were scarred, *bad*. I do not understand this. This has got to be one of those miracles I have heard about."

The doctor looked at me and stated in a strong voice, "You knew. No one could shake you. Not even your pastor could change your mind. How did you know? Tell me. How did you know? I have had other doctors tell me about seeing miracles with some of their patients. Some said there had been a very quick healing, which was very unusual, but this is my miracle boy. Tell me, how did you know?" The odd thing was that he kept asking the same question, "How did you know?" He never once gave me the opportunity to answer him.

This doctor wanted Garry to stay with his bandages off in a dark room for twenty-four hours, slowly allowing his eyes to readjust to light. He wanted to check my son's eyes again before he would let him go home. This was fine with me. This was the proof. Garry's eyes had been severely burned, but now, through a miracle of God, his eyes were completely healed.

I had to get to a phone to tell Bob. He needed to know immediately what the doctor had said.

I went to Garry's bedside. I explained to him again that his eyes were all right and what the doctors were going to do. It was the first time since the grease fire that I had seen him smile. I held his hand as we talked about his miracle. He knew God had healed his eyes. My son had his eyesight restored. God is very good and loves us very much.

Now let me tell you what happened to both Bob and me.

What I Experienced

The doctor removed all the bandages and told Bob and me that Garry's eyes were all right. Garry was sitting up in bed. The room was still partly darkened. The hall lights were reflecting into the room, and the bathroom light was on. Garry had one more night to stay in the hospital. This night would be different from the others, as he knew his eyes were all right.

Garry told me to go home so I could sleep in my own bed. I had slept in a leather chair with big wooden arms for three nights. He told me I should go home and check on his older brothers. He didn't need taken care of anymore, but his older brothers did, he said. He had his great sense of humor back, and started to tell the nurses his never-ending series of jokes. The nurses all said they would take good care of him. "Go home and get some rest," they said to me.

That afternoon, I told Garry I would not be back that night. I would be there the first thing the next morning, I said. Then we would go home once the doctor released him.

I went directly home. I was tired, but it was a great feeling. I talked with Bob and the boys for a while. My big mistake was in lying down across the bed. I zonked out. I slept all evening and all night. Bob and the boys went out to eat that evening. They also went to the hospital to visit with Garry.

When I awoke the next morning, I looked out the big picture window across the room from the end of the bed. I was looking at the four electric lines and at the one large cable that carried the telephone service. Sitting on the electric wires and the phone cable were doves. They were sitting side by side like birds in a shooting gallery. Each dove was sitting close to another, each of them spaced about three inches apart on every line. The lines were completely filled with birds. I just lay there looking at them. All of a sudden it finally came to me that there were far too many doves. Doves usually travel in pairs. You will generally see one or two at a time. Doves do not sit like that on a line, and yet here were five lines full of them.

As I took a closer look, I saw that each dove was just like all the others. They were all a pure white color with a soft gray patch under the wing. They were all the same size. I shook Bob and told him to wake up and look out the window. "I never have seen anything like this before. Look at the doves. They are sitting on every line. Every line is filled with doves," I said.

Bob got up, looked out the window, and went downstairs. I heard him yell, "You haven't seen anything yet. Go look out the windows all around the house."

I jumped out of bed and looked out the window. Doves were all over the yard. There were hundreds of them. They were spaced only about ten inches apart. There were also doves on the fence. The most unusual thing was that they stopped right at our property line. There were no doves in the neighbors' yards; instead, the neighbors' yards were full of blackbirds. There was not one blackbird mixed with the doves. It looked as though someone had set a huge clear plastic case over our home and yard, from boundary to boundary.

The boys and Bob were up watching the birds, running from window to window just as I was doing. Bob yelled at me to look out the back of the house. I ran to the bedroom window on the other side of the house overlooking the backyard. I saw doves, hundreds and hundreds of doves. I couldn't believe what I was seeing. They were all over the diving board, on the fence, on the top of the light pole, and everywhere else I looked. The doves, as previously mentioned, were all the same size and were a brilliant white with a light gray patch under their wings.

I ran downstairs to look out the living room window. I really wanted to see the doves up close. When I ran up to the window, they did not even move. They were sitting on the windowsill. If any other type of birds had been sitting there, they would have flown away from my movement. This was another true miracle of God.

After I put my hand on the window, a dove turned its body sideways and then turned its head toward my hand. I just leaned against the window and watched all of them. I was absorbing everything I could about what was happening. There were now thousands of doves. Praise God. Hundreds of blackbirds were feeding in our neighbors' yards all around us. I didn't want to take my eyes off of this spectacular sight.

The telephone rang. What a time for the telephone to ring! I ran around the corner to the kitchen and grabbed the receiver. "Hello," I quickly said. It was my aunt. After telling her I would call her back in a little while, I hung up.

I raced across the living room and went back to my window to watch the doves. My heart sank. They were gone. There was not one bird anywhere. I ran out the front door. I saw no sign of one bird anywhere. Both the doves and the blackbirds had completely vanished.

I couldn't have been gone for more than ten seconds. With that many doves, you'd think I would have heard the flapping of wings had they taken off in flight. They could not have flown away so quickly. Bob and I walked out into the yard. There was no sign of bird droppings. This truly was a miracle of God.

What Bob, My Husband, Experienced

On the evening when Garry's eyes had been burned, Bob prayed and prayed. He called everyone he knew and asked them to pray for Garry. He called several pastors and asked for the prayers of their church congregations. He called his brother, Harold, who was the pastor of a church in California. Harold had been at his congregation's midweek prayer meeting. He called his brother-in-law in Owasso, Michigan, and asked him to ask his congregation to pray. Many people were praying that night for Garry. Bob got everyone he could think of to pray.

As Bob was walking around the pool and praying, he felt God's peace come upon him as he had never felt it before. This was approximately 10:30 p.m. He knew that he had God's assurance that everything was going to be all right. Garry's eyes were going to be all right. Garry's eyes were going to be healed.

He had to tell me what had happened. He couldn't call me, so he drove back down to the hospital to tell me. Once he was inside the hospital, he took the elevator. When the elevator reached the floor I and Garry were on, Bob got off and then started to walk down the hall. When he saw me, he came running toward me and said, "It's going to be all right." We learned that God had spoken to us at the same time, revealing that Garry's eyes were healed.

We talked, crying tears of joy.

After Bob and I left the hospital to head home, the Devil started to torment Bob, saying, "You're an educated man. Miracles like this do not happen today. It is just wishful thinking on your part that Garry's eyes are healed. You know that Garry is going to be blind, so just accept it." The Devil was trying to plant doubt in Bob's mind.

When we arrived home, Bob went to the backyard and prayed more earnestly than he had ever prayed before. At 3:00 a.m., he was exhausted. He said to God, "I believe you, but would you give me a sign to verify the healing of Garry's eyes?"

The following morning, I woke Bob to see the doves on the electric lines. He went downstairs and looked out the big picture window in the living room. He saw hundreds of doves feeding in the backyard. This was God's way of saying, "Here is what you asked for."

He went to the kitchen and looked out. There were doves, hundreds of them. Next door in our neighbors' yard were hundreds of blackbirds. They were huge, all of them feeding in the neighbors' yard. Bob looked next door to the east at our other neighbors' yard. Their yard was full of blackbirds too.

There were only doves in our yard. This was the sign from God that Bob had asked for.

Kerry and Bob Jr. ran from window to window upstairs, trying to take in all of the birds. Bob Jr. was captivated by the doves that were sitting on every windowsill in the house. They never made a move to fly away, not even when he walked right up to the window. The boys were captivated by the birds.

We all saw the traffic stop on the road. People could not believe what they were seeing. Cars just sat in the road, afraid to move for fear of scaring the birds away.

Later that morning, the bandages were removed from Garry's eyes. His eyes had healed.

What Happened to Me after the Miracle

A few weeks later, I needed to have my eyes checked. Garry happened to be home with me that day, so I asked him if he would go with me. The two of us pulled into the full parking lot of the eye clinic. I thought we might have to wait a while to see the eye doctor. We walked into an office waiting room where several people were waiting. The nurse told us that the doctor had gotten an emergency call to head to the ER and was now on his way back. Garry and I looked at one another and smiled.

The doctor walked in and spotted Garry right away. He almost yelled, "You are my miracle boy." He proceeded to tell everyone there what had happened to Garry. He wanted to hear the story about his eyes again. And then I told him about the doves and the blackbirds. The doctor said to me, "I believe everything you have told me." He said to Garry, "Never forget what God has done. You are going to use those eyes to benefit humankind."

The doctor made it a big point to tell us that he had started going to church and had accepted Christ as his Savior. He told us that he had opened a Saturday-morning eye practice and was giving all of the proceeds to the Lord. He was still talking about his miracle boy to a lot of his patients.

I still get tears in my eyes when I think about the wonderful miracles God has given me and my family. He is always with us. He hears every prayer.

Jesus tells us to ask, believe, and receive.

Garry finished junior high school and high school. He received his degree in clinical laboratory science from Indiana Wesleyan University. He continued his education in this field at Ball State University and Huntington College. I would definitely say that Garry has used his eyes to benefit humankind. Thank you, Lord.

Big Tornado

Marion, Indiana
May 1965

In May of 1965, a tornado crossed the state of Indiana. It traveled miles without lifting off the ground. It was a mile wide when it traveled through Marion. We were told that there were twin funnel clouds and that they traveled together as one huge storm.

On this particular Sunday evening, a tornado warning had been issued, but a newscaster had just come over the Indianapolis station to give us the all clear. I looked off toward the west and saw that there was a storm that looked black and dark purple and that was traveling very low to the ground. It was a mean-looking storm, one of the darkest I have ever seen. It was quite a distance from our house. I thought to myself simply that all the storms tracked to the northeast. We probably wouldn't be affected at all. I just dismissed it from my mind.

We had some company drop in for a short visit and then leave. Bob then went outside to drive the truck up the drive.

I returned to my bedroom, where I was finishing a term paper. I was also studying for an exam I was scheduled to take the next morning. Garry and Kerry were right behind me. We were laughing about something. The next thing we knew, Bob was yelling my name frantically. "Betty," he said, "open the door." He was beating on the front door and yelling at the top of his voice. At the same time, I began to hear a low roar. At first, I thought it was a train that I was hearing. The roar got louder and louder.

My mind was thinking several things all at once. Some of my friends had been through a tornado. They had all said that at first the tornado sounded like a train.

At this point, the sounds became much louder. My friends had said that in a case such as this, one had no time to do anything but take cover.

Kerry and Garry were upstairs talking with me. I screamed, "Get downstairs." They didn't hesitate. The three of us bounded out of the bedroom. Garry, at my left, had a tight hold on my skirt. Kerry was right behind me, hanging onto the back of my blouse with a tight grip. The lights went out. It was now pitch-black. We could not see anything.

As we were racing down the stairs to the living room, we began to hear the house ripping apart. Bob had been screaming at the front door. The door was to the left at the bottom of the stairs. I tried to open the door so Bob could get in. I and the boys were in the foyer. I yelled at the boys to go downstairs to the family room.

The roar was so deafening that they hadn't heard one word of what I said. The wind was so strong that it felt like sand was beating me in the face. I was thinking about getting someplace where the boys would be safe and about helping Bob get back into the house.

I grabbed the doorknob and turned it, but the door would not budge. Bob was pounding and pushing on the door as I was turning the knob and pulling on it. The air pressure had changed so rapidly that the house was sealed like a pressure cooker.

Our roof ripped off. The rock wool insulation started beating us in the face. I reached for the doorknob again. Once I turned it, the door flew open very easily. But Bob was not there. When I opened the door, Kerry had thought I was going to go outside, so he passed me and ran out the door. I grabbed for him, but his shirt just slipped through my fingers.

Bob came in through the door. He and Kerry had passed one another but hadn't realized it. It was pitch-black outside, and the roar of the storm was deafening.

I screamed that Kerry had gone out. Bob started out to find Kerry. Kerry bumped into him when coming back in. Talk about a nightmare. We all raced downstairs to the family room, finally all together. Bob Jr. had been in the family room throughout the whole storm.

The air pressure was so great that we could hardly breathe. After a few seconds with all of us standing together in a huddle, the tornado finally passed. The silence we now experienced was just the opposite of the deafening roar. The air was almost too still.

The roof that had been over the kitchen was now gone. We stood in the foyer and looked at the stars, which were once again shining as though nothing had happened. We couldn't walk around to see any damage, as it was too dangerous to do so. We made our way to the truck, which still had its windows. The five of us piled in.

We checked one another over to see if anyone had been hurt in any way. Bob had cuts on his arms. We kept three posts in back of the flower box that was outside our front door. He had wrapped his arms around two of those posts to keep himself from being picked up and blown away. The edges of the posts had cut into his arms where he had held on tightly. Bob said that the storm had lifted his feet off the ground. If it had not been for the posts, the funnel cloud would have sucked him away.

We had friends who lived about a mile from us. They came and took the boys home with them. Bob and I sat in the truck trying to make a few decisions about what to do. He said, "How do you feel about all this mess?"

My reply was, "It all belonged to God before he allowed us to have it. It is his to do with as he pleases. We are all okay. God will take care of us."

God had spared our lives. I was very thankful that God had kept us safe throughout the most horrendous storm I had ever been in. That was the most important thing, as life cannot be replaced. I learned through all of the terror that material things just do not matter.

My father, mother, and sister, who lived across town, had been listening to the radio. They had heard the roar the storm had made. They heard the news report on the radio that the nearby Three Acres Trailer Park had been completely destroyed, so they knew we had been hit by the tornado. They drove as far as they could. The police would not allow them to drive any closer to the disaster zone, so they had to walk several blocks to our place. The closer they got to our home, the worse it looked. Phyllis, my sister, was yelling, "Betty! Are you there? Are you all okay?" Bob and I called out to her, saying that we were okay. She had run from the trailer park and was out of breath. We yelled for my parents to slow down and rest.

One of our friends came looking for her husband. She had gone to church with her mother-in-law that evening. She said that if we saw her husband, Pete, we should tell him she was fine. Their home was completely gone. Nothing was left of it.

Whereas Pam was looking for Pete, Pete was in a panic looking for Pam. We heard his voice frantically yelling for her. It was coming from the field behind us. He thought that she had been blown away with the home.

We flashed our flashlights and all yelled to get Pete's attention. He finally saw us. He laughed and cried. Then he almost collapsed from the fear and anguish he had been feeling.

Bob and I decided to leave the truck and take the car. If we could make it to the end of the road, we could turn left and get out of the mess. We finally made it out, after which time we picked up the boys and went to my parents' home for the night. There was nothing we could do about our home until daylight.

The next day, we had quite a shock. We wondered how any one of us had gotten out of our house alive. The bedroom that the boys and I had been in was now totally caved in. If we had not gotten out immediately, we would have been killed. When Bob put his hand against the bedroom wall, the whole wall started to fall out. We had made it out just seconds before everything started happening. The kitchen had no ceiling at all; it had all been sucked out. The living room had half a ceiling, as half of it had collapsed into the room. The rest of it was gone. The dining room had no ceiling at all.

The only thing that had not been damaged in the whole house was the fireplace, which was located in the middle of the house in the living room. The contractors stated that it had acted like a huge spoke. This could have been part of the reason why the whole house had not blown away.

There was glass all over the foyer. It had blown in when we opened the door. One of the boys had been walking across the glass barefoot. Thanks to God's hand of protection, his feet did not have one little cut. Isn't God good?

The Second Tornado

Bob and I bought a pull-type camper to live in while contractors were rebuilding our house. Two weeks after the tornado, I was wakened when the camper shook from one side to the other. I jumped out of bed and ran to the window. Guess what? There was a tornado going down the same path that the other one had taken. This one was a much smaller tornado. I could see inside the twister. It was not black as the other one was. Instead, it was light brown in color. My eyes fastened on a big box that was swirling around and around in the huge funnel cloud.

I lost it. I was screaming. The camper was lifting off its wheels, first on one side and then on the other. Finally, it stopped moving.

From then on, I listened to every weather report. If showers were reported, I would become nauseated. Even little white clouds made me uneasy. This went on all summer. I kept praying about it.

Later, in the fall of that year, my eldest son, Bob, and I were in the front yard watching a storm come toward us. It had passed over the airport and was coming straight at us across the field to the southwest. I saw low-lying clouds about five hundred feet above the ground. For some reason I was not scared like I had been during the other storms. I made myself stand and watch until this storm was about a quarter of a mile from our home.

Bob yelled, "It's time to get in the house, Mom. Come on!" He pushed the button to close the garage door. We ran to get to the lower level of the house. I was amazed at what I saw, something that stopped me dead in my tracks in the living room. The water in the swimming pool was rising to form peaks about six to ten inches high all over the water's surface. At the top of each peak, a ball of water about the size of a golf ball was forming. These were being thrown out of the pool toward the west.

The antenna tower was twisting, bending, and creaking, creating the sound of metal pieces grinding together. "There goes the antenna again," I yelled. There was a difference about this storm, though. God's peace was upon me and I had lost that horrible fear. I had prayed and prayed for deliverance from that awful fear. I realized I was not queasy in my stomach, my hands were not trembling, and I did not have that feeling of panic. I was amazed at a few of the things I was seeing. I had laughed when saying, "There goes the antenna again," because that was the third time we had lost our antenna tower that year. God had taken all my fear away. As God's Word reads, "I am with you always."

September 1965

In the fall of 1965, I had become very tired. Trying to get back into the house was a real job. I had new curtains and drapes, and we needed to replace furniture, fixtures, carpet, and a great many other, little things. I was teaching school all day and then coming home to do all the things that should have been done yesterday. I was beat. Day after day I did this until I felt I could do it no longer.

This particular morning, I rolled out of bed feeling just as tired as I had been when going to bed the night before. I felt as though I had reached my limit. As I was on my way to school this October morning, I said, "God, what good is all this? Up at 6:00 a.m., race all day, drop into bed at night so exhausted that I toss and turn all night long. I am so tired that it feels as if I haven't gone to bed at all."

That evening after returning from school, I went into the living room and dropped to my knees near the footstool. After praying a short while, I lifted my eyes and saw that my Bible was lying there on the stool. I opened it. Immediately my eyes fell upon this verse:

> It is a fearful thing to fall into the hands of the living God. But call to remembrance the former days, in which, after ye were illuminated, ye endured a great fight of afflictions; partly, whilst ye were made a grazing stock both by reproaches and afflictions; and partly, whilst ye became companions of them that were so used. For ye had compassion of me in my bonds, and took joyfully the spoiling of your goods, knowing in yourselves that ye have in heaven a better and an enduring substance. Cast not away therefore your confidence, which hath

great recompense of reward. For ye have need of patience, that, after ye have done the will of God, ye might receive the promise. For yet a little while, and he that shall come will come, and will not tarry. Now the just shall live by faith; but if any man draw back, my soul shall have no pleasure in him. But we are not of them who draw back unto perdition; but of them that believe to the saving of the soul.

Hebrews 10:31–39

No one can deny that God gave me this Scripture just when I needed it. Thank you, Jesus.

Archway of the Little White Church

Summer 1971

I feel that in every Christian mother's heart is the great desire to know that her family is saved. The following is a wonderful vision that Jesus gave me to provide me with assurance that my family was saved.

I was above a city, in the Spirit, looking down on a very busy street. There was an small old-fashioned white wooden building sitting in the middle of some new tall and gleaming structured buildings of several stories. Cars and trucks were noisily speeding toward their respective destinations. Crowds of many people were hurrying to go somewhere. It looked as if it were a rush hour in the middle of a great business district, with all the hustle and bustle of crowds and traffic.

As I looked upon this scene, I noticed that every once in a while a person would turn and enter a plain little white building. Each person who entered was seemingly in a hurry to go there. I wondered why more people were not going in. I felt an urgency for people to go in, even though I did not understand why they were going in. I remember thinking, *Why are all the others too busy or in too much of a hurry to come in?*

It was then that I saw my son Kerry come hurrying down the walkway amid the crowd. When he came to the little white building, he turned in. With big long strides, he reached the large double doors and took hold of the big handle on one of the doors. After he opened the door and went inside, the roof atop the little church vanished. I could see everything that was inside it.

There was a small foyer just inside the doors. Three very wide platform steps, carpeted in a royal red, led through a wide archway. It was an old-fashioned one-room church with a foyer.

As Kerry hurried up the steps, my eyes beheld Jesus, who was standing in the archway. As Kerry went up to Jesus, Jesus held out his hand. He took Kerry's hand and then put his other arm around my son's shoulders. Jesus said, "I am so glad to see you, Kerry. Go right in. It is almost time." Kerry walked through the archway and into a room that seemed to be filled with white clouds.

I then saw Garry coming down the street. He definitely was in a rush and knew right where he was going. He hurriedly turned in and went through the big double doors. He also hurried up the red-carpeted steps and went straight to Jesus. Jesus took Garry's hand and put his arm around him. He said, "I am so glad to see you, Garry. Go right in. It is almost time." Garry walked through the archway and into the room filled with white clouds.

When I looked up the street again, I saw Bob Jr. walking down it. Bob had the walk of a person who knew how important it was to hurry and arrive at this special place. He was determined to be there as soon as he could get there. He turned at the walkway and went through those huge wooden doors. He almost ran up the red-carpeted steps to Jesus. Jesus took hold of Bob's hand and put his arm around him, just as he had done with Kerry and Garry. Jesus said, "I am so glad to see you, Bob. Go right in. It is almost time." I could see Bob Jr. walking through the archway and into the cloud-filled room.

At that instant, I was walking and half running with my husband, Bob, down that same crowded sidewalk. There was a difference, though. We were coming from the other direction. We were hurrying, moving as fast as we could go, weaving in and out through that crowd of people. We turned once we reached the sidewalk and then went through those big double doors. We walked quickly up the carpeted stairs to Jesus. Jesus took hold of Bob's hand and my hand at the same time. He told us how happy he was to see us. Then he told us to go right in, as it was almost time.

My husband and I walked into the cloud-filled room and immediately went up to Bob Jr., Kerry, and Garry, who were talking together. We were now all together. Our destination was heaven.

God has been so good to me. What a promise he gave me with this vision. God wanted me to know that my family was saved. *I praise him.*

"I Said Stop!"

Summer 1972

After school one nice summer day, I settled back against the seat of my car and was enjoying my drive home. I was traveling north on Sand Pike Road, just before my turn onto Fiftieth Street. I was going across a small bridge at the bottom of the hill that was approximately 250 feet from the corner where I normally turned off.

As clear as if it had come from someone sitting right next to me, a voice said, "Stop." I jerked my head around to see who had said it. There was no one anywhere around the car. Again, I heard the voice. Clear and firm, it said, *"I said stop!"*

I applied the brakes immediately and stopped the car. I was about a hundred feet from the corner, sitting there and trying to figure out what was going on. I looked around to see if anyone was watching me. If there had been anyone, then he or she would have thought that I was loony for stopping where I had.

There was a man sitting in his front yard at the house on the corner. I remember thinking that this man had to be wondering why I stopped where I had. His house sat on a street corner and was high up on a hill. It blocked the view of traffic on Sand Pike Road unless you were right up next to the road that turned off.

There was a big farm truck in the opposite lane, driving in the other direction. As the truck approached the T intersection at Fiftieth Street, a car come speeding out of Fiftieth Street and drove directly into the path of the farm truck. As the car tried to make a sharp left turn, it took out the Dead End sign and a few others with it. The car came very close to rolling over.

My attention went to the trucker who had been forced off the road to keep from hitting the car. He had the right side of his truck on a steep embankment, having come very close to rolling the truck over on its side. Once he got the truck off the hill, he swerved clear over to my side of the road. He was headed straight toward me. He swerved back to his side of the road, trying to get his truck under control. He passed me on his side of the road and then came to a stop behind me. He was partially on my side of the road. Had I gone on to the corner to make my turn onto Fiftieth Street, I would have been killed. The car would have hit me on the driver's side. The truck would have hit me with great force. It would have been a three-vehicle crash that would have killed all of us.

The man at the house on the corner said that he had seen what happened. He had expected it to be a terrible crash. He was amazed at what had actually happened, though. He told the police officers the story. He kept asking me why I had stopped. Because I had stopped, all our lives had been spared.

I know what happened. My guardian angel had been riding with me. God gave me words of instruction that provided for my safety. I praise God for the fact that I heard those words. And I learned a lesson: be obedient and act swiftly. I praise God and thank him for watching over me.

Hysterectomy

August 1974

I was admitted to the hospital on August 22, 1974, to have a complete hysterectomy. The doctor started me on hormones at this time. I took this medication until 1979.

Beginning in the spring of 1978, every time I opened the package containing the new prescription of pills, I was drawn to read the long sheet of warnings included in the package. A sheet of warnings was included with every prescription I had purchased before, but I had not given any of them too much of my attention. I asked my doctor about the warnings for this particular medication, and he told me not to worry about them. I would be on these pills for the rest of my life, so I was rather concerned. For years I had not been worried about any side effects from my medication, but now the warnings and the list of side effects were of great concern.

I tried getting off of those pills. If I refrained from taking them four or five days longer than the normal seven days, then I had feelings as though I was dying. My doctor called these feelings hot flashes. Because I was struggling with the hot flashes, I would start taking the hormones again. I could not stop taking them. No matter how hard I tried to stay off the pills, I felt that I had to have the hormones that my body was not producing anymore.

My family and I went to see relatives of my husband on a Sunday for some special event. While I was there, Uncle Doc gave me thunder for being on the hormones. Then Bob's cousin told me she had suffered through those hot spells without taking the hormones.

After that, I tried harder not to take the pills. I was determined to get off those things. I had been praying about it.

Going to church was very special this Sunday morning. As I listened, I heard the minister say, "If you have something you cannot conquer yourself, come to the altar." That invitation was meant for me. I knew that it was for me. I went up and knelt at the altar. I simply told Jesus that I could not get off the medication on my own. I had tried hard, but now I needed his help. Would he please help me so I would not need to take any more of the medication?

The next week went by very quickly, as I was flooded with work. I suddenly realized that I had not taken the hormones for one whole week. I did not need them anymore.

Isn't God good? I had tried for one year to quit taking the hormones, but God got me off them after one Sunday morning's worship service. I believe that God was teaching me that I have to give up and surrender all to him. I had to tell him I could not do it myself. It is when we surrender that God gives us the miracle or shows us his great hand of protection.

I look back on this experience in my life and relate it to the kids of today who take street drugs. They need help. God's help is the only answer. He is in the deliverance business too. My God can do anything and everything. It is up to the individual who needs the help whether or not to ask him for it. Call on him. God decided to wait for me to give up before he delivered me. When you totally surrender to God, you recognize that God has things worked out for your good all the time. God had it all worked out for me. He is never too early or too late. He is always with you. He is always on time. He is my God.

Gift of Christmas Carolers

December 24, 1977

It was near Christmas. People were buying gifts, trimming trees, and wrapping presents. Everyone in my family was trying to find out what I wanted for Christmas. They were continually asking me, "What do you want for Christmas?" My reply was always the same. There was nothing I really wanted. There was nothing I needed. I have never been a person who wanted everything they could see. I had a nice home, nice clothes, and all the necessities of life. I truly needed nothing. This is what the peace of God does for a person.

After several times of being asked this same question, I stopped and thought for a minute. "I would like a choir of angels to sing to me," I replied. Then I added, "How beautiful that would be to hear heavenly angels sing as they do in heaven."

The following is what happened that Christmas Eve.

I heard carolers singing Christmas carols. I ran to the front window to see them. To my amazement, I saw no one there. I continued to hear the singing, this time a little louder than before. I ran back through the house and looked out the kitchen window. I saw no one. The singing was beautiful. I did not want to miss the carolers who had come all the way out to the country to sing to me. I threw open the kitchen door and ran into the backyard. I still saw no one.

The moon was full and huge in the sky. It was so bright that it lit up the outdoors—like a giant light bulb in the sky. The moon and stars looked so close that I could almost reach up and touch them. I had never seen the sky so clear and beautiful. Again I heard the carolers. When I turned to my right, my attention was drawn upward. There was a choir of angels above me in the heavens. They were slowly walking down toward me.

They were standing in midair as though there was an invisible slanting floor beneath them. They were not standing as an earthly choir would stand. They were grouped as one would stand a set of ten pens. The back row had five angels, with four more angels in front of those. Three angels were standing in the next row, and then two, and then finally one angel. This last angel was the leader.

This was the most beautiful choir I had ever seen or heard. The angels were singing the whole time they were walking down out of heaven to come toward me. They stopped and stood a very short distance away from me, still standing in midair.

I had always thought of an angel being a beautiful woman, mainly because angels always seem to be depicted as such. This choir of angels were all men. Each angel was dressed in a royal velvet robe. Each one wore a different-color robe. Deep purple, gold, royal red, burnt orange, chocolate brown, forest green, and royal blue were the colors, and they could have been made only in heaven. The rich colors lent a majestic feeling, leading me to think that I was in the presence of a choir of men who were very close to God.

Each angel was different in height and size. Each one wore a crown, but each crown was different. Each angel had his hair intertwined with his crown. Some crowns were very tall. Some were wide and tall, and others were shorter. All of the crowns were different sizes. Every crown had jewels of all kinds. Huge stones were in some of them, surrounded by smaller stones. Some of the crowns had many large and medium-size cut stones. Some were shorter and had many smaller stones. Each of these crowns was loaded with hundreds of the smaller stones. And each crown had been made specially for the particular angel on whose head it sat.

The angels were singing a Christmas carol the whole time they were walking down from heaven. They stood and sang the most beautiful song I have ever heard. When the angels finished singing that carol, they started to sing "Joy to the World," my favorite Christmas carol.

The angels started to move slowly backwards. They turned around in unison very slowly as if they were all one body. They were leaving. They began walking back up into heaven while singing "Joy to the World." I did not want them to go. I thought, *How do you call to an angel to stop? You do not yell at them, "Stop, angels! Come back!" How do you call to them to stop them from leaving?*

All of a sudden I was calling, "Michael, don't go! Please, come back!" The first angel turned around slowly, parted ways with the group, and walked down to where I was standing. I was holding my hand out, my palm up, trying to reach up to him. Michael held out his hand with the palm down and touched my hand very lightly. He slowly backed up a few steps, turned around slowly, and walked back to take his place among the group. They sang "Joy to the World" all the way back up into heaven.

I stood there and watched as they went higher and grew smaller. The singing became softer and softer. The angels finally disappeared, completely out of sight. When I could see them no more, the singing was completely gone.

I stood watching the stars and said to myself, "God, you are so good to me." It was the most beautiful night I have ever seen. There were no clouds in the sky. The moon was a huge lighted ball. The stars were all shining brightly. I thought to myself that the stars had lit the path for the angels as they came from heaven and then returned. God had given me the second best Christmas gift I had ever received. The very best Christmas present was the Lord Jesus, who was born in a manger. God sent his Son so that we might have life in him and eternal salvation.

I love you, Lord. You do so much for me all the time. Thank you for loving me so much.

If you are saying to yourself, *I don't know if God loves me,* know that he has already proven to you that he loves you. He gave you Jesus, his Son. Jesus has already given his life for you. It is up to you now to make the decision of accepting him as your Savior or not.

Second Vision of Christ

June 15, 1980

My arms were in pain and my bones were cracking. I had pain in my head and joints. Awaking at 11:00 p.m. and going downstairs, I picked up Bob's Bible. I prayed and asked God to use my life in the time I had left. I wanted to do his will in winning souls for his kingdom. Also, I needed deliverance and healing.

I opened the Bible and turned randomly to Matthew 4:23–24, which reads as follows:

> And his fame went throughout all Syria: and they brought unto him all sick people that were taken with divers diseases and torments, and those which were possessed with devils, and those which were lunatic, and those that had the palsy; and he healed them.

God had spoken to me through his Word. All I could do was just praise the Lord. I knew that I knew. He was telling me in his Word that he was going to heal me. I didn't know how, when, or where. I just knew that this was his Word and his promise to me. I thanked him for his love and care for me. I praised him for healing me, and then I went back to bed.

At about one o'clock in the morning I had a vision. There was a huge room. I had never seen anything like it before. Very elegant, with white pillars and a ruby floor, this gigantic room had no ceilings or walls. There were three long platform steps that ran the whole length of the room. There was a red plush carpet that ran to the building and covered the steps. There were six white marble pillars spaced around the floor. I knew somehow that this was a building, one made of white marble and a giant red ruby.

Jesus was standing at the top of the steps. He was captivating to behold. His white gown glistened. His hair glistened too, and a soft glow radiated from his whole body. There seemed to be a light that made everything shine and glimmer. Jesus is the most beautiful sight that your eyes can ever behold. His smile held so much love and compassion. He was very glad to see me, and I was very glad to see him, as he is my life. Indeed, he is everything to me.

I was standing at the bottom of the steps on the red carpet. Once Jesus opened his arms to me, I opened my arms and ran up the steps to him. When he put his arms around me, I put my arms around his waist. I felt safe and secure as a little child might feel when seeing someone she loves. Then my hands fell to his side where he had been pierced with the spear. All of a sudden, I felt ashamed. I stepped back.

Jesus was standing there looking at me. He was speaking to me, not audibly but to my mind. He said, "I died for you. What are you doing for me? You have been standing on all the promises and receiving all the blessings."

This statement rang through my mind. I tried desperately to think of all the things I could say I had done. I had taught Sunday school classes and Bible school classes. I went out with witnessing groups. But I still found myself very ashamed. I had to answer, "Nothing, Lord."

Jesus said, "I made you. I know everything you have done, everything you are doing, and everything you are going to do." I realized that everyone someday would have to stand before the Lord. I clearly understood what Jesus was telling me. He then led me to a huge chair that had what looked like a white sheet on it. He pulled the sheet around me and then looked me fully in the face. He said, "I will pray to God the Father for you."

I thanked Jesus again and again. I awoke thanking and praising Jesus. I praise his name. He has done great things for me. I will stand before him someday. I do not want to hear him say, "You have done nothing." I want to hear him say, "You have done well."

I did not understand what Jesus meant when he said, "I will pray to God the Father for you." I was to learn later what this meant.

At my church, we formed witnessing teams and went out to witness, covering the whole town of Marion. Many people whom we visited accepted Christ as a result. What a thrill! We went out of town to other churches for a weekend and taught in those churches, saying that the people there should do the same as we were doing and witness in their own towns. I had never before felt this much on fire to go out and witness to others about the Lord Jesus.

In the following chapters, you will learn, as I learned, what Jesus meant when he said, "I will pray to God the Father for you."

Healing of Lupus

January 1981

I had undergone a series of blood tests when I was in my late twenties. My doctor said that my white blood cells were a little bigger than my red blood cells but that it was nothing to worry about. In my later years it could become a problem for me, he said. He told me that he would keep an eye on the situation.

This problem had completely slipped my mind after a few years had passed by. The doctor I had seen previously was now dead. As a result, we had no family doctor. Bob thought we should have a family doctor, so I made an appointment with a new doctor for a checkup, scheduling it for January 1979. Once I saw that doctor, he said that he wanted to start me on antibiotics right away. He asked, "Did anyone ever tell you before that your white blood cells are larger than your red blood cells?" He went on to explain the abnormal size relationship between my cells. He seemed very concerned about it.

I thought, *I have known about this for almost thirty years. It is nothing to worry about.* My new doctor suggested that I make the earliest appointment available to have a series of tests done. I did not make an appointment, completely dismissing the matter from my mind.

One year later, in December 1980, for some reason I seemed impressed to have a series of blood tests run. The doctor was concerned about the results of my blood tests. He wanted me to make an appointment to start antibiotic treatments right away. I could not take antibiotics because they made me suffer horrible side effects. I think that the prospect of side effects scared me more than the abnormal white blood cells did. I had put off taking antibiotics because of that fear.

After my appointment, I came down with the flu. I had never had it so bad. It settled in my lungs. I sometimes would scream in pain when I coughed or sneezed. I made an appointment with the doctor. I knew he was really going to let me have it for not having gone back in to see him.

I was told again that my white blood cells were very large and also that I had abnormally small red blood cells. He then said that I was going to get over the flu as soon as possible. Next, he and I were going to get to work on this other problem.

My family had been planning to go to Florida over Christmas vacation. The doctor said that it was okay for me to go. "It might do you a lot of good to get some sunshine while you're down there."

The pain had eased some. It no longer made me cry out. My family and I went to Florida. My doctor had given me strict instructions:

I was to call him the minute I returned home. I returned from Florida on Saturday, January 10, 1981.

One day soon thereafter, Bob Jr. came home about noon. I told him about a young man I had seen on TV whom God was using in a miraculous way. Bob said, "Hey! I saw him too." We talked about the young man. Both Bob Jr. and I wanted to go to one of his church services, so we both said, "Let's go."

Bob, my husband, came in at that point and sat down at the kitchen table. He wanted to know what Bob Jr. and I were up to. My son and I asked my husband if he would like to go to Cincinnati. He replied, "We have to go up north to pick up the half cow we ordered."

Very determined, I replied, "Bob, every weekend we always do things that have to be done. Just this once, I would like to do something I really want to do." I simply felt certain that I had to go to this service.

Bob said, "We should go pick up the meat, but I guess we can go to the service."

The three of us went to the service that night. We saw God working through the young man. We saw many miracles. In fact, we received a blessing for going to that meeting.

We got home that night at about 2:30. The trip had taken three and a half hours, but we were all glad to have gone.

I taught my Sunday school class the next morning and attended the morning worship service. After lunch, I said, "If I wasn't so tired, I would like to go back to Cincinnati for the service tonight."

Bob Jr. said, "I'd like to be there tonight too."

Bob Sr. added, "I would like to hear his sermon."

I was getting tired and weak. I did not know if I could make the trip. Bob said, "You can lie down and sleep. Bob Jr. and I will do the driving." They wanted me to go back and be there for the evening service. We all agreed I needed to go.

We drove back to Cincinnati to attend the evening service. We saw many people healed, and we praised the Lord for his work. After the pastor ended the service, several people had on their coats and were starting to leave. All of a sudden, the pastor ran back to the pulpit, grabbed the microphone, and yelled, "Wait a minute! Everyone sit down. I thought that God had finished, but God is still speaking to me." He waited a couple of minutes until things calmed down and people were in their seats again.

The pastor looked down and pointed his finger straight at me. He said, "The lady in the blue velvet jacket: do you know a Betty?"

I replied, "Yes! That is my name."

"God is speaking to me. He has a miracle for you. Come out to the aisle. I will meet you there," the pastor said, almost yelling the words.

The pastor asked me, "Have you ever talked with me before?"

I answered, "No, sir."

He asked, "Have you ever talked with anyone connected with the church and told them of your medical need?"

I said, "No, sir."

The pastor then said, "God has a miracle for you. You have been having sharp pains in your head and eyes."

I said, "Yes."

He said, "You have been having dizzy spells and light-headedness lately."

I said, "Yes."

He said, "You have weak spells. You get very tired and shaky a lot lately."

I said, "Yes."

"God is allowing me to look inside you. You have trouble with your hemoglobin. You have a very bad infection right behind your eyes. God is going to heal this. This is causing the pains in your head. I am now looking into your bloodstream. Your white blood cells, or corpuscles, are greatly enlarged. They are double the size of your red corpuscles. You have an infection in your bloodstream. Your whole body is full of infection. God has said that all of this infection in your bloodstream is fatal for you if not treated within a very short time. God wants you to have this miracle," he very sternly stated.

The reverend started to stretch out his hand to pray for me, but then he pulled it back. He said, "You are to go back to your doctor and have more blood tests run. The test results will all be normal." He stood quietly for just a moment, and then he said, "Here is your miracle." He reached his hand upward and touched my forehead. My body went limp under the power of the Holy Spirit. My mind was fully active. I could hear everyone around me praising the Lord. I could hear the pastor and the people singing. In my mind I was saying over and over, *Thank you, Jesus.*

Bob, Bob Jr., and I arrived home around 2:30 a.m. I got up at 6:00 a.m., went to school, taught all day, came home, and had not noticed the difference in me. I looked at the housework that needed to be done since I had played hooky all weekend. I did some dishes, folded clothes, put the clothes away, and cooked some dinner.

My husband was sitting in the big easy chair in the living room, smiling. "It's 10:30 p.m. I think we had better turn in. It has been a long day," he said. That was when it dawned on me that I had not been tired all day. Isn't God good? This was the first evidence of God's healing miracle in my life.

I called the doctor's office. He wanted to admit me to the hospital immediately to run a series of tests and get me started on antibiotics. I asked him if it would be possible for me to do the tests as an outpatient. I did not want to lie around in the hospital waiting for the outcome of the tests. I knew I did not need to do that because I had been healed. Very reluctantly, my doctor allowed me to have the tests done as an outpatient. He would call in a prescription for an antibiotic for me to get started on.

Early Tuesday morning I went to the hospital to have the series of blood tests I needed. Boy! The phlebotomist took several vials of blood. I asked if he was going to leave me any. Everyone laughed.

I called the doctor's office around four o'clock on Thursday evening. His nurse said, "Please wait a minute. The doctor wants to talk to you." She then came back to the phone and said, "The doctor is tied up right now, but he said he wants to talk to you. He wants you to make an appointment with him and to get to the hospital now."

I asked, "Can you tell me if any of the test results are in?"

She said, "Yes, two of them came in." I asked her if she could tell me about them. She said, "Both tests show normal, but those tests do not really tell us what we want to know."

I said, "Praise the Lord!"

The nurse said, "What?"

I told her that I would find out when I could get off from work, and then I said that I would call her back tomorrow. I did this to buy time until some of the other test results came in. How do you tell a nurse over the phone (especially one who is aggravated at you) that the Lord Jesus has healed you?

I called the office again on Friday, but no more test results had come in. This nurse was very good at her job. Again she insisted I make an appointment. I promised her I would do so when more of the test results were in.

I called back on the next Monday. I got the receptionist on the phone this time, as the nurse and doctor were both busy. No test results had come in.

I called Tuesday. The nurse very curtly said, "One more test result has come in." She mentioned that I should stay on the line, as the doctor wanted to talk to me.

I thought, *Now I am going to get it.* I admired the nurse a great deal. She was trying to do her job, and I probably was a real problem to her. She came back to the phone in a short while and said that the doctor was busy with a patient. He wanted me to know that the sediment test had shown normal. I said, "Praise the Lord!"

The nurse very curtly asked, "What?" Then she stated that the doctor wanted me to wait until two more test results were in. I should make an appointment after they were all in, she informed me.

I called on Thursday. No test results had come in. I called on Friday. No test results had come in. It was another long weekend. I was very anxious for all the test results to be in, even though I knew what the prognosis was going to be.

God is very good. I could have gone into the hospital, but if I had done so I would have wasted good time and lots of money. I do not know if the doctor would have believed me. The doctor might have started me on antibiotics right away, going by what the previous test result had shown. I wanted to have the test results before telling him my story.

God works out everything just right. I called the doctor's office again on Monday at noon, this time from the school. The nurse said that the doctor wanted to talk to me but he was with another patient. Could I please call back, or could he call me later when he was free? I explained that I was teaching and would be home by 4:00 p.m. I asked if the nurse could tell me the results of the lasts tests to come in. She left me on the line and shortly returned. Evidently she had needed to get permission from the doctor to tell me the results. She said, "Mrs. North, all of the test results are in, and they are all normal."

I said, "Praise the Lord." I was waiting for the nurse to say "What?" again. This time she fooled me. I praised the Lord all the way back down the hall to my room. All my test results were in. They were all normal. Those were the words the pastor had used when he said, "Go back to your doctor. Have all of the tests run again. All the tests will be normal."

I went directly home after work. As I was turning the key in the lock of the door, the telephone began to ring. Once I answered, I found that it was the doctor's nurse. She asked me to please hold the line for just a moment.

The doctor came on the line and said to me, "Betty North, I am so happy for you. It would be a waste of your time and a waste of my time if you were to make an appointment now. All of your test results are normal. This is a complete switch from the first tests that were done. You knew. I don't know how you knew. I am so happy for you. Every test result is normal."

I said, "Tell me about the white and red blood cells. What size are they now? What do they look like now?"

He replied, "They are normal, Betty. The cells are normal."

He said he would like to talk to me about what happened. He wanted to know all about it in detail. Now, however, he had patients he had to get back to. Again he said, "I am so happy for you."

All the evidence was in. What I had known by faith was now visible. God gave me a great miracle. God touched me and healed me. I now had the proof that some would need to believe me when I witnessed to them about my healing.

I had been praying, "God, have me in the right place at the right time to do your will." When I was praying that prayer for others, I did not know that God was already working in my life for my own healing.

A year Later, I had the chance to tell my doctor all about the miracle. He said, "I was putting you in the hospital with less than three months to live. You had the faith for your healing."

God rarely does anything in the way that you think he will. He does it in his way and in his time, never leaving any doubt that it was a miracle from God. Remember in the last chapter when Jesus said, "I will pray to God the Father for you"? This is what he prayed for. He is our intercessor. He prays to God for us.

I keep in my purse the little drawing that the doctor had made for me of my blood cells. He drew it on one of his prescription pads, not knowing I would be able to use it as proof when I was witnessing about my healing. The drawing shows the size of my cells and what they looked like when I had lupus. It serves as a reminder to me of God's mercy and grace. It serves as proof to every doubting person who questions my healing. God healed me of lupus. I praise you, God, and I give you all the glory. Thank you for the miracle of healing. Your Word says that you will never leave us.

A Sunday Service

The first Sunday after all my blood test results had come in, I was heading out the door of my house to go to church. The phone started to ring. My first thought was to just go ahead and let Bob answer it, but I decided to go back inside and answer the phone.

It was a friend of mine. She said, "I have heard about what has happened to you, and I think it is wonderful. I have something to ask of you. Our minister was called out on an emergency last night. We have no one to take our morning service. Would you come and tell the people about your healing and take the morning service?"

I replied, "I was just going out the door to teach my Sunday school class. I don't see how I could possibly do it."

Like a bolt of lightning, clear as a bell in my mind, I heard God say to me, "You said you would never say no!"

I very quickly changed my answer to my friend's question, saying, "I will be there as soon as I can get away after class." I didn't know how God was going to work this out, but it was going to be interesting to see. God would not have said what he had said to me if he did not want me to share my experience at the service.

I hung up the receiver and raced to church to teach my Sunday school class of fifth-graders. The second my class was over, I ran to my car. I had fifteen minutes to get to the small country church, five miles west, where I was to speak. Once I arrived, I swung the car into the parking lot and ran for the church door. An usher who had been waiting for me to arrive was standing at the door. He very quietly slipped me into the end seat that had been reserved for me.

The church ushers were taking up the offering. The next thing I knew, someone was introducing me. All of a sudden, sheer panic set in. *What are you doing here? You have never before spoken to a church full of people. What are you going to say to all these people?*

As I passed the man who had introduced me, he said, "You have thirty-five minutes." I had figured that what I had to say would take me five minutes, ten at the most.

Panic. I cannot even begin to explain the panic I felt at that moment. I felt as though my knees had turned to rubber. I took hold of the podium and faced the church full of faces. I told the congregation how happy I was to be there, saying that I felt it was the Lord's will that I was there.

I started telling the story of my illness. The words just seemed to flow. Some of the words I used were not part of my normal vocabulary. I knew I had finished my story when I simply had nothing more to say.

I thanked the congregants for having me come to speak to them. This had been the most wonderful opportunity to witness for the Lord I had ever had, I said. I felt elated. As I walked down from the platform, descending the stairs, I looked right smack into the face of a big clock hanging on the side wall. The time was exactly twenty-five minutes after eleven. I had talked for thirty-five minutes exactly.

The church members then had their closing song and prayer. They were dismissed at 11:30, their regular dismissal time.

I praised the Lord. What happened in that small country church that day was 100 percent the Lord's working. I think it was his way of testing me. Jesus wanted to know if I would do what I had said I would do. I'd received the phone call from my friend at the last minute. I'd had no time to prepare anything. I'd had no time to think of what I was going to say. It was the first time I had ever spoken to a large congregation. God left no doubt in my mind that the whole thing was totally his doing.

I thank God for using me in the way he did. He has shown me that when he wants to use us, what matters is not what we say or do, but what God says and does through us.

What an experience! Praise the Lord!

One Year Later, after Lupus

January 7, 1982

One year prior, I had picked up a virus just before Christmas vacation. I had remained sick until my lupus was healed on January 10, 1981. This was the first time I needed to go back to the doctor.

One year prior, God had touched me and healed me of lupus. At that time I did not have the opportunity to share my testimony with the doctor.

A year later I had a routine examination. The absence of Lupus was confirmed. After he had examined me, he started to excuse himself in order to get to his next patient. He then stopped and drew a deep breath. He was tired.

I asked him, "Doctor, did you ever wonder how it was that my test results were initially so bad but then, once you had the whole new series run again, they came back normal?" He whirled around, came back, and sat down on the stool next to me. I stated, "I know you are very busy. I do not want to keep you from your patients. Would you have just a minute for me to tell you about what happened?"

The doctor said, "Yes, I want to know all about it. Don't leave out one thing."

As quickly as I could, I told the doctor about my trip to the church in Cincinnati, Ohio. I told him all that had happened there, especially about the pastor pointing me out at the end of the service and saying, "God has a miracle for you. God is allowing me to look into your bloodstream. Your white blood cells are enormous compared to your red blood cells."

"That is exactly what you told me my test was showing, isn't it, Doctor?"

He replied, "Yes, it is."

"The pastor told me that God was saying that if it were not for the miracle I was receiving that night, my condition would be fatal in a very short time." I asked, "Is that true, Doctor?"

He replied, "Yes, it is."

I then told him how the pastor told me to have all the tests run again, and that God had told him every test result would be normal.

The doctor said, "You had the faith. I have had a few other patients tell me how they had been touched by God and were healed. They gave God the credit."

The doctor went back through every test. He explained all the tests that were run and what each result meant. He named one of the tests as the critical one, mentioning that it had read 1/60, which was dangerously high. He said the normal reading for that test was 1/40. I did not understand everything he was saying, but I tried to absorb everything I could from our conversation. The one thing I did understand was the short amount of time I had had left on planet Earth: less than three months. My lupus had developed to the critical stage. There was no slowing it down or turning it around.

The doctor then said, "I am of a different faith than you. You are a Christian and you have faith." He then said something that totally surprised me. "I have two daughters in my family who are dying of lupus."

I thought he was speaking of two actual little girls that were his daughters. I asked, "You have daughters dying of lupus?"

He then explained, "My young patients are my daughters. The older women are my sisters. All of my patients are members of my family."

This had been a very profitable office visit. I had gotten to share with my doctor what had happened to me. He thanked me and told me that I was a true witness of the fact that God had healed me. All of the people who had been involved in the testing could not figure out how the big change in the test results had come about. The results for all the tests that had been run on me had gone from critical to normal.

The doctor called me a few weeks later to explain that one young girl, age seventeen, had a short time to live, just as I had had before. He asked if I would please write down the name of where I had attended the church service as well as the name of the pastor. The doctor stated that he could do no more for the girl. He said, "I am going to give this information to her. I do not know if she is a Christian or if she is of any religion, but I am going to tell her of your faith and your healing."

I wanted the doctor to know, if the girl was interested, that he could give her my name and phone number. I would be glad to talk with her. He explained that he had to keep things anonymous because of the laws protecting patient confidentially. I had been happy that I had gotten to tell the doctor what happened to me, but to know that my miracle was being passed on to a seventeen-year-old girl who was dying made me even happier.

Jeremiah 30:17: "'For I will restore health unto thee, and I will heal thee of thy wounds,' saith the Lord."

1 Peter 2:24: "Who his own self bare our sins in his own body on the tree, that we, being dead to sins, should live unto righteousness; by whose stripes ye were healed."

Isaiah 53:5: "But he was wounded for our transgressions, he was bruised for our iniquities: the chastisement of our peace was upon him: and with his stripes we are healed."

There are many promises of healing in the Word of God. When we put on the armor of God, we put on God's protection. When we need healing, God is our healer.

Read your Bible. In fact, buy yourself a small Bible that can be slipped into your pocket or carried in your purse or tote bag. This way, the Word of God will be at your fingertips. It will also be in your heart and in your mind. Having a little Bible allows you to quickly share the Word of God with someone who does not know it.

I have shared with many people what God has done for me. God's Word touches the lives of many who need to hear his promises. When God does something great, such as making a miracle happen for you, he wants you to share it with others.

Clown Dream

June 17, 1983

In this dream about clowns, Bob and I were at a place of entertainment, sitting inside a huge building that was like a large gym or an auditorium. We were at a live show, laughing at some of the performers' antics.

All of a sudden, out from behind the stage curtain came a man who gave the impression that he was a comedian or a part of the clown act.

There was a woman, heavy-set with many physical problems, sitting next to me. This man pointed to her and said, "You are sick. Come out here. I am going to heal you." She went out to him. He put one of his hands on each side of her head. I cannot remember what he said to her, but I do know that there was neither any glory given to God nor any credit given to Jesus. There was no mention of God or of Jesus throughout the entire dream.

All of the spectators present were standing in a long line. This man then walked down the line. He stopped right in front of Bob and me. I shoved my hands up and pushed my arms out in a posture of defense. I said, "Don't you touch me. You can do nothing to me. I am a Christian."

God was showing me that it was not by his power that this man was working miracles. I had been praying for God to show me what was right and what was wrong, as I wanted to know the difference.

The Holy Spirit was not in the building. God's name had not once been used. The name of Jesus had not been spoken either. This was a place of entertainment, and here this man was promoting himself as a healer. He was taking the glory. On top of that, he had the power of evil working in him. The people were clapping and laughing. As I looked from face to face, I realized that these people had no idea of what was happening. I knew, though, that we were not ever going to see God heal someone by way of a person in an entertainment venue who was trying to elicit hilarious laughter. This so-called healer was not a godly person.

Jesus made clear to me the difference between what is right and what is wrong. God does not share his glory. He gets all the honor and all the praise.

Lord God, we give you the honor. We give you all the praise. We give you all the glory. We thank you for your miracles, which are given only by you.

Heaviness of Evil

Spring 1989

Our preacher was in the beginning stages of implementing a new program of prayer at our church. He wanted prayer groups, prayer partners, prayer chains, and prayer warriors who would sign up to pray round the clock from Saturday to Sunday until it was time to attend church. He stated that those who decided to take part in this prayer group would be attacked by Satan. I had never heard any pastor warn people that this would happen. Until that day, it had never crossed my mind that something like that would happen.

I had signed up for one hour, from two o'clock to three o'clock every Sunday morning. I knew this would be hard at first, but I was quite surprised to find that I could do it with ease.

When my alarm went off at 1:55 a.m., I bounced out of bed and slipped on my robe. By the time I got downstairs, the phone was ringing. My caller was the person who had been praying in the time slot before me. We prayed together for a bit, and then I hung up the phone and prayed alone for the rest of the hour. At three o'clock, I called the next person who was to start praying.

I enjoyed this time in the morning to pray. It was very quiet. It was like a new world had opened up to me, one that I had never experienced before.

A few weeks passed. I had not thought any more about what the pastor had said about being attacked. I went into the spare bedroom and sat down at my desk to pray. I had been praying for a short time when a feeling of heaviness started to move into the room. It got heavier and heavier. I could hardly breathe. The heaviness was starting to squeeze me. I firmly said, "Satan, I bind you in the name of Jesus. Get out of here and leave me alone. Go."

The heaviness started leaving. The pressure lessened little by little. I could feel it leaving the room. Soon it moved completely out, which is when the words of the pastor came back to me: "Satan does not like you praying. He will try to scare you into quitting."

I thank my God that I belong to him. God is all-powerful. I praise him and give him all the glory. My prayer time grew and grew. Prayer is a powerful key to our walk with the Lord.

Entrusting a Dream to the Future

November 1989

This was one of those dreams that make you wake up in a cold sweat with your heart pounding wildly, as if you had just run ten miles.

As usual, I woke my husband to relate to him what had just happened. In my dream, he and I were amid a large gathering of people. We were talking and laughing with lots of acquaintances and friends. Everyone was dressed for the occasion. All were putting their best foot forward.

Slowly something began to happen to the person I was talking with. Her face began to twist and take on a very grotesque look. I turned my head away and started to look around the room. There were other faces taking on that same horrible look. I soon came to realize that 80 percent to 85 percent of the people in the room had this horrifying look.

They continually looked from one to the other and smiled. I was thinking that they were saying to one another, "How long will it be before the others break down too?"

I was horrified. All I wanted to do was to get out of there as fast as I could. I looked around for Bob. He was talking and laughing with a group of people. Seven or eight of them had this monster look, but Bob was not seeing it.

I wanted to scream at him. I wanted to yell, "Bob, stop talking and come on. We have got to get out of here. These people are not our friends like we thought. I am seeing the way they look. This is what they truly are in their hearts." I kept quiet, though, because I didn't want to let my peers know that I was seeing them as they really were.

There were a few others in the room who had not taken on the hideous look. Each one was surrounded by some of the evil ones. The evil ones seemed to have a purpose, trying to lead those whose features hadn't changed to do things they should not do.

I kept yelling in my mind, *Come on! Come on!* I wanted to scream to warn the innocent ones, but I could not. I dared not appear in any way that would allow the hideous ones to know how I was seeing them. It might mean that I and the other innocents would be killed. Here were friends whom Bob and I had known for many years. Many were people we trusted as Christian friends. They were caught up in it. I knew which people we could trust and which people we should no longer trust. The latter group were now of the Devil.

Then I was wide awake. I was saying out loud, "We are too trusting. We need to be on our guard. What does all this mean?"

In my mind, it was as though I knew the answers to my questions. I have always been too trusting. I have often believed what people have told me. I trusted people at their word. I knew there was a time coming when we Christians would not be able to trust many people at all. God was showing me discernment. God was showing me whom to trust and whom not to trust. If we put all our faith and trust in God, then he is with us.

Sin will become more and more prevalent in the coming years. The best of Christians will fall away because of their complacency. Pastors will fall. As it stands now, temptations assault us by way of the news media, TV, books, and magazines. Filthy films shown on TV and in movie theaters bombard us from all sides. Violence is put into the hearts of people, including the hearts of children, as a way of life. Children are growing more disobedient, cruel, and unfeeling, making the home a place for verbal and physical battles. The love of God is no longer in many people's hearts.

You will look upon people's faces and listen to their speech. Worldly pleasures, greed, lust, and self-satisfaction will take over their conversation. We among the faithful must keep walking with the Lord. We must stay in the Word. We must pray and keep trying to live a holy life.

Don't let others put you down. If unkind words are said about you or to you, turn the matter over to God. If others have taken advantage of you, lied to you, or lied about you, give the matter to God. The Lord will take care of the problem much better than you ever could.

Same Corner, Third Time

Summer 1990

I had taken my mother out of the nursing home for a little while. We had gone to Walmart and were on our way back home. I had stopped at the mobile home sales lot to tell Bob something and was now on my way back to the van.

I was getting into the driver's seat when a voice in my head said, "Pray." I did not hear it with my ears; instead, it was very clear in my mind as though it had been spoken aloud. I told Mother to sit there for a minute while I prayed. I prayed for a safe trip to get her back to the nursing home and for my safety in returning home. That was what seemed to be on my mind to pray for. That was what I was involved in doing at that time.

I started the motor. After a few minutes of waiting for the traffic to clear, we were on our way. I took a shortcut down Fiftieth Street and was nearing the hill that became a dead end street after the turn onto Sand Pike Road.

I had a very healthy regard for exercising caution at this corner. As I neared the corner, I slowed down to a very slow roll and eased the van along. There was a blind spot that obstructed my view to the right. This was caused by the hill of the property on the corner. I applied my brakes and came to a full stop. The next thing I saw was a car turning the corner, cutting it way short. The car was coming at me head-on. The woman who was driving slammed on her brakes and stopped her car a hair's width from my bumper. She was looking straight up into the van and smiling. I guess that when you do something stupid like turning into the wrong lane of traffic to cut a corner, offering a smile is all you can do. The woman put her car into reverse and backed out onto Sand Pike with cars coming both ways. She did not even look for traffic first. I was gritting my teeth, expecting a wreck of some kind. Out loud, I asked myself, "How do some people get a driver's license?" The woman pulled ahead, steering the car just enough to move past me and make it onto the other side of the road. As she passed by me, she smiled again. I could not believe that we had been an inch away from having a head-on crash before she had stopped two lanes of traffic to back out into the road in front of the other cars. All this woman could do was smile when she finally got around the front of my van.

Then I remembered the strong voice in my head: *"Pray."* I praised the Lord all the way to the nursing home. God had known what was going to happen. He had wanted me to pray and ask for his protection. Jesus sent his angel to stop the smiling woman from crashing into me. Isn't God wonderful to us?

If God puts a very strong thought in your mind, *be obedient and act on it.* If it is something for you to do, *do it!* If God says for you to pray, then *pray*. If God puts someone on your mind, then *pray for that person!*

This was my third big incident on this corner. I thank God that I was not alone for any of them. God was with me every time. He had total control of the situation.

When you are in the middle of an impossible situation that is out of your control, remember that nothing is impossible with God.

Three Black Cats

This particular day was a special one for me. I had finished most of my household duties early. Bob had gone for the day. I decided this was a great time to pray and read the Bible.

I was sitting in the dining room at about 5:00 p.m. I had spent a great deal of time reading the Bible and praying. I looked out the glass doors and across the backyard, and was reminded of all the doves I had seen in the yard the morning after Garry's eyes were healed. I was thinking out loud, saying, "It would be nice to see a couple of doves in the yard."

I returned to reading the Bible. It seemed as though the people and the events described in the Bible had come alive on this particular day. I just did not want to quit reading. I heard a rustle just outside the door. I had set a big black plastic bag of trash outside for Bob to carry to the can when he came home. I just knew the dog next door had gotten into the backyard and was trying to get into the bag. I turned in my chair to get up and was shocked at what I was seeing.

There was a huge black cat sitting just outside the screen door. It was three times the size of a normal-size cat. It was shiny, was jet-black, and had huge orange eyes that seemed to be glaring at me. It was as though the cat was looking right through me and might pounce on me any second by jumping right through the screen door.

I realized all of a sudden that behind this cat were two more just like it. The two paced back and forth for a short time and then sat down near the door and glared at me as the cat in front of them had done. I knew that these cats were evil. This occurrence was something very abnormal. Each of these cats was almost the size of a small leopard. All three had shiny, coal-black hair with huge, piercing eyes.

There was no doubt in my mind that these were not normal cats. I knew that this was an act of evil. I also knew that this cat by the door was going to act. It was as if I had to do something quickly. The cats were getting ready to pounce on me right through the screen. This was something Satan was doing.

I pointed my finger at the first cat, the one sitting right next to the door. I felt that it was getting ready to spring on me, that it was going to come right through the screen. It would have been nothing to the cat. I said firmly and in a strong, commanding voice, "I bind you, Satan, in the name of Jesus Christ. Get out of here in the name of Jesus."

I was shocked when the cat flipped around and shot out across the backyard. It ran all the way back to the neighbors' barn, going so fast that it left a blur behind its body. I knew this cat was of Satan. The cat did not become transparent or disappear. The cat did not run away. It shot through the air like it had been fired from a gun. It left a trail like a fog, or like thin white smoke, behind it. As it was shooting through the air like a rocket, the trail was right behind it. I believe that God allowed me to see this to know how fast the cat was moving.

My attention was drawn back to the two cats that had been sitting behind the first one. Both cats were sitting like statues glaring at me. I was very angry now. I had to move fast. I pointed my finger at the second cat. With all the power and authority Jesus gave me, I demanded, "I bind you." Pointing to the third cat, I said, "And I bind you in the name of Jesus." With a wave of my hand, I commanded, "Both of you, get out of here in the name of Jesus." Both cats flipped around and were jet-propelled away as fast as the other cat had fled.

I knew that what had just happened was supernatural. I asked aloud, "Lord, what does this mean? Why did this happen? What do you want me to learn from what just happened?"

I heard no audible voice, but in my head the answer was there, as though someone had spoken it aloud. "I allowed this to happen so that you would know that three people are coming against you."

I had gone through a season of feeling hatred and bitterness. It was as if I knew that I was now going to undergo a time of testing. Would I hate? Would I grow bitter again? Would I resent the things that were happening? I had to keep my eyes and ears open to know what was going on. I had to be on my guard to protect my soul.

I knew I had to have God's intervention. I prayed for God to help me. God had shown me what to do: bind and command in the name of Jesus. I prayed with faith for God's intervention. With God's help, I would not hate, become bitter, or let resentment take over my life.

God was teaching me to bind and command in the name of Jesus. He was teaching me to let him do the work. I was to pray. He was teaching me to praise and worship him for all that he was doing in my life. It is not by our power that we do anything. It is by God's power. He gets the credit. He gets the glory. We are never to share in it. We are to give him all the praise and all the glory. Praise his holy name.

White-Feathered Wing

March 1997

I had taught school all day and had just come home from a CAP (Civil Air Patrol) meeting. It had been a full day. I was tired, having just dropped into bed. I ached from the top of my head to my toes. Suddenly I felt very alone. I cried. I said, "Jesus, I feel so alone."

The room was in total blackness. I looked up. Hanging over my body was a huge circle of white feathers, solid white feathers that were whiter than white. It was the most beautiful thing I have ever seen. The circle started slowly spreading out, getting larger. I just watched it, trying to drink in the beauty of it and of what was happening. Slowly the feathers continued spreading out into a huge wing. The wing was longer than my body. It hung over my body for a small period of time. I could feel a peace and a quietness that were both very noticeable. The circle of feathers formed a large wing that started to lower very slowly. It stopped about ten to fifteen inches above me, covering my whole body. Then I fell asleep.

The next morning, I felt very refreshed after having had a wonderful night of sleep. I was not tired, nor was I dragging through breakfast. I had more energy than I had had in a long time.

God is very good to us. As Psalm 91:4 reads, "He shall cover thee with his feathers, and under his wings shalt thou trust."

Driving while the Choir Is Singing

September 25, 1998

I had gone to the altar one Sunday, and there followed the Lord's close presence all week.

One particular day during this week, I had been praying. I was headed for Atlanta, Indiana, to visit Bob Jr. We were going to spend the next day at the big Atlanta street fair.

I said another short prayer just before leaving home. I got into the car, backed out of the garage, and was on my way. I went west to the four-way stop sign and then started to turn on Highway 37 South. Just then, I began to hear the singing of a very beautiful-sounding choir. At first it was very soft, very faint. I thought it was coming from the radio, so I punched the volume button, but nothing happened. I then pushed the on/off button. I was testing the radio, trying to figure out why it wasn't working. I pushed the on/off button again and the radio came on, blaring loudly. I quickly pushed the button again to turn the radio off. I now knew the radio was off.

Where was the music coming from? It had gotten a little louder. The choir sounded very beautiful. I didn't think I had a cassette tape or a CD in the player. I touched the eject button for the tape player. Nothing ejected. There was no tape in the tape player. I touched the eject button for the CD player. Nothing came out. There was no CD in the player. And as I previously mentioned, the radio was off.

The choir was getting louder and louder. My head seemed to be full of the beautiful music. Then I started noticing that there were no musical instruments. There were thousands of voices singing very beautifully. Then I knew what was happening: God was allowing me to hear this beautiful heavenly choir. They were singing to the Holy Spirit.

There was a tremendous difference in the meaning of the words, I discovered, compared to what I had always known them to be. The choir members were singing one song over and over, never changing to another song. The song they were singing over and over was "Holy Spirit, You Are Welcome in This Place."

Before, when I had sung the song myself (which was many times), I had been telling the Holy Spirit that he was welcome to come to this place, the place where I was residing. It was a song of invitation. It was a song inviting the Holy Spirit to abide with me.

I listened very carefully to the feeling that was coming from the voices singing the music now. They were not inviting the Holy Spirit to be with them. He was already there. They were singing a joyous song of proclamation. They were telling the Holy Spirit how thankful they were for His being there with them. They were telling Him how welcome He was for being there. He was with them, and they were making him welcome. As a matter of fact, he was there in the car with me right then. I joined in the chorus thanking the Holy Spirit for being with me.

I do not know how many times the choir sang the same choruses to the Holy Spirit and to me. I began singing with them, and then I began to cry as I was saying, "Come, Holy Spirit." As the choir was singing praise to him, the Holy Spirit's presence become very strong. The Holy Spirit's presence was with me. I trembled and cried. I wanted to pull over, but there was no place for me to do so.

I heard the choir all the way to Greentown. It started to get a little softer with each chorus. By the time I had reached Greentown, I had to listen ever so closely. I could still tell what they were singing. Next I could only hear parts of phrases, and then I couldn't hear anything. I suddenly began crying very hard. I just sobbed. I cried hard all the way from Greentown to Kokomo.

I pulled into Shoe City. Bob Jr. was sitting in his car waiting on me. We were going to get something to eat before going to the fair. I pulled up by his car. He knew there was something wrong. He quickly hopped out of his car and came over to my window. I had tears all over my face, my face soaked from the crying. Indeed, I was still crying.

Bob asked, "What is the matter, Mom?"

I said, "I'll tell you about it as soon as I can stop crying." He just stood there for a few minutes. I dried the tears, gained back a little composure, and proceeded to tell Bob what had happened.

Bob smiled. He said, "God has given you many visions, dreams, and miracles in your life. God loves you."

I said, "Bob, I feel like God is getting ready to use me in some very special way." We talked for a while about how the Holy Spirit is going to be poured out onto God's people. Many, those who are complacent, indifferent, and self-seeking, always thinking that everything is going to happen tomorrow, will miss it because they are seeking things, worldly pleasures—and everything in their eyes is about self, self, self. The Holy Spirit is pouring out his love. He is here; it is happening today.

The following Sunday, the pastor at my church asked for people to come to the altar if they wanted to be filled with the Holy Spirit. I went to the altar on September 20, 1998, and asked the Holy Spirit to fill me with himself, as much as I could stand. I wanted to know him. I wanted to know all about him. I wanted to be able to talk with him when I had a question or needed him. I wanted him to teach me. I wanted him to convict me if I went to say or do anything that was not right in God's eyes.

If you do not want it, don't ask for it. If you ask in faith, believing the Holy Spirit will work in your life, then you will receive it.

God knows your heart. He knows if you really believe what you are asking for.

You should pray to God, praying what is in your heart.

God wants his children to draw close to him. The Holy Spirit will help you draw close to Jesus and to the Father. Welcome the Holy Spirit into your life.

John 15:26: "But when the Comforter is come, whom I will send unto you from the Father, even the Spirit of truth, which proceedeth from the Father, he shall testify of me: 'Holy Spirit, you are welcome in this place.'"

Wall of Fire

This was one of those sleepless nights. I was up every hour or two throughout the night. It was going on 6:00 a.m. and I was still fighting to go to sleep. I was very tired, drained of strength.

I was sitting on the edge of the bed. All of a sudden I was compelled to go look out the front window of my bedroom. I pulled back the drapes and saw the most astounding thing happening in my front yard. There was a huge wall of fire, four to five feet tall, clear across the front of the house—a brilliant red blaze with no smoke at all. It was a neatly trimmed hedge that was a blazing fire. I watched it for a long while before turning away. When I looked back, it was gone. I went to bed and lay there for a short time trying to figure out what had just happened. Guess what? I went to sleep. Can you imagine that? I lay down and went to sleep.

Visions of God are very peaceful. I have never felt afraid while having one.

The wall of fire had appeared in my front yard. I could not determine what it meant.

It was on my mind, off and on, for the next couple of weeks. Every time I walked out my front door, I envisioned the hedge of fire in my mind.

What were you telling me, Lord? There are times when the Lord tells me the purpose for a vision right away. There are other times when I have to wait a little while for the understanding to come. But one thing I learned a long time ago is that I should put my full trust in the Lord. He is never too late and never too early; instead, he is always right on time. Trust him.

Fingers of Smoke

September 8, 1999

I awoke around 3:00 a.m. I knew I was not going to get back to sleep, so I decided to get up. Sometimes in the middle of the night I go down to the living room and read the Bible or pray. Most of the time I do both.

I was passing the big window in my bedroom. I reached over, drew back the drapes with my hand, and looked out. I was shocked by what I saw. I stood there watching what seemed to be moles tunneling right toward the house. I could not count how many there were. It was like the fingers of both hands were slowly coming toward the house. The fingers reached clear across the front yard. It was as though they were on fire under the ground. I did not see the fire, but I could tell it was there from the dark gray smoke coming from the fingers as they moved toward the house. The fingers looked like moving molehills.

I knew that this was evil. I felt uneasy. Something told me that a lot of bad things would soon try to come at me. My pastor had told my whole witnessing group that Satan would not like what we were doing. We were going out in pairs to visit people's homes and talk about their accepting Jesus as their Savior.

I wondered about the vision of the wall of fire that the Lord had previously shown me. I was praying for the Lord to reveal to me the meaning of what I had seen.

The Lord revealed the meaning of both visions. This is what I understand them to mean. The first vision was about God's protection. The second was a warning of trouble.

The hedge of fire was God's protection. It stretched clear across the front yard to protect me from the trouble that was about to come. Each one of the gray smoking tunnels headed toward the house would be completely cut off by the hedge of fire. God was going to protect me from all of them.

I started having trouble, taking hits from every direction. God was with me at every moment. He had wanted me to know what was coming. He also wanted me to know that he was the judge and I was not to take matters into my own hands. God took care of some of my problems so easily that I was amazed. When the problems presented themselves as one of those fingers of smoke, God cut the evil off at the wall of fire. Every person and every situation that came against me, God changed for the good. God told me to not pass judgment on them, as I am not the judge. Rather, he is the judge—the only one—and his judgment is true. God told me not to reply with anger or to say anything back to people who spoke against me. I was to remain silent and to watch as God worked everything out.

Psalm 91:8: "Only with thine eyes shalt thou behold and see the reward of the wicked." God had been making miracles happen for me. He was teaching me to keep my mouth shut, not to reply to anyone who confronted me or denigrated me. I was tired of the things people did to me once I became a widow.

God is the only judge. If I wish to defend myself or to take over and decide to retaliate by mouthing off, God will let me do it. But I choose to turn these matters over to God. Making this decision and putting it into practice was the hardest thing I have ever done. But to get myself through, I kept reciting Psalm 91. The verses of that psalm were coming true in my life. Only with my eyes was I seeing the rewards of the wicked.

I was not happy to see some of the things that were going on. I was learning from Jesus. He was working with me and teaching me how I needed to walk as a Christian. I also learned that I was to turn all of my problems over to him, as he would take care of them for me. He also gave me a choice to retaliate against people. But Jesus kept reminding me that he is the judge. I was not to judge people who harmed me. I was to pray for them. This was a great lesson for me.

Many times when things look tough or impossible, remember that with God all things are possible. He continually tells us that He is with us. He wants us to put all of our trust in him. Keep in your heart and mind always the question, if God is for us, who can be against us? I choose to turn everything over to God.

Go—A Vivid Dream

August 10, 2004

Very early in the morning, I had an extremely vivid dream. I took part in the entire thing. At times I felt as though I was actually living what I was seeing. The dream was in color. Its major purpose was to warn me about the future so that I would be protected and my life would be delivered from destruction.

At the beginning of the dream, I was in an old farmhouse that sat back from the road. Its wooden exterior was badly in need of a fresh coat of white paint. Even though I did not see the drive, I seemed to know that it was made of crushed white rock.

I was standing in a large living room and looking out a big picture window. The scene outdoors was beautiful. It filled the window like a huge painting. It was late spring; I could tell from the different shades of green. Some trees were a deep green. They looked almost like velvet. The trees were in a huge woods that ran from the back of the farm all along its west side. There were fields, approximately one hundred acres in size, behind the house.

There were also approximately one hundred acres to the west of the house, separating the house from the woods. Don't ask me how I knew it was west; I just did. There were medium shades of green on the younger trees, and a very light green on the smaller trees. I stood there taking in the beauty. Different kinds of trees were different shades of green. Each species had its own color. The new crops coming up in the fields had their own shades of green.

The sun was shining. It was a beautiful day. The farm was very well kept. From the window I could see that the yard was a beautiful soft green.

I knew there was a woman in the room with me, but I did not see her. She explained that she had to check on something in the back of the house. I heard her walking down a short hallway, and then she was gone.

My attention was drawn back to the window. I could see that a storm was coming. It seemed to be traveling in a long front line from the southwest, all across the west, and extending as far as the eye could see to the northwest. With a huge front line, it was the meanest-looking storm I had ever seen. It was very unusual. With most storms, you can see the clouds rolling and churning at the front. This storm's line seemed to be closer to the ground than usual. Already huge, it was getting bigger and darker. It passed over the wooded area, and then it began to roll on the ground. It grew in height and now seemed to tower hundreds of feet into the air. The roll of clouds seemed to change into a monstrous roll of destruction filled with swirling fine black dust that emitted light in an array of colors: yellow, blue, green, rose, and purple, with random flashes of bright light. As the storm cloud approached, I could clearly see a fence-like structure of enormous size rolling upon the ground with metal wiring as big as a tank tread. As the storm slowly approached, it seemed to destroy everything in its path.

I was looking intently out the window. The woman ran through the hall from the kitchen and then grabbed the doorknob to a door that went to the basement. She yelled as she went through, "I am going to the basement. It is safe there." I still did not see her. I had had my back to her when she ran by. She didn't ask or tell me to come with her.

At the same time, a huge figure of a man came through the kitchen door and stepped into the hall. It was the clothing he was wearing that made him appear to be huge. In reality he was a normal-looking, average-size man, but he was wearing a type of black biological or chemical suit. I tried to see through the face mask of the helmet. I could see no face because the shield of the helmet was smoky gray in color. The man walked stiff-legged. His arms were not at his sides because of the puffy suit he had on. He walked up the hall toward me, stopped, and entered the living room. He turned to face me directly and said in a very stern, demanding voice, "If you are on medication, grab your medicine and *go*." With his arms, he pointed in the direction that I should go: east.

I quickly responded to his command. He had given me an order. I followed his orders because I knew he was trying to save my life.

The woman was never mentioned or thought about again. My purse was in my hand. I ran to the front door and opened it. I ran to the car, got inside, and backed out of the drive onto the road. As I was shooting forward down the road, I looked into the rearview mirror. I was pulling away from the storm. I was beginning to feel peace, knowing that *everything* would be all right now. This was the end of the dream.

Two Flat Lines, One Big Heart Attack

On Thursday, November 4, 2004, my son Bob called from his home and told me he was coming up to take me out to lunch. The Lord had wakened him to say, "Go and see your mother," but Bob did not say a word to me about the Lord sending him to my home until much later.

Bob's position at the Tipton Hospital as a medical lab technician had changed his lifestyle tremendously. He worked the night shift and therefore slept during the day. That morning, around 11:00, he called and asked me if I wanted to go out for lunch. My reply—yes—was quick, as I love to go out and eat whenever I have the opportunity.

By the time Bob got to my house, I was having some pain in my back. He said, "Let's go down to the emergency room and have it checked out."

At the emergency room, the staff ran several different tests on me. One of the ER doctors, a cardiologist, came alongside my bed and said to me, "You are having a heart attack right now. We are taking you to the cardiac floor as soon as you can be moved."

On Friday (the following day), I was on my way in an ambulance to a heart center in Indianapolis. My sons Garry and Bob followed the ambulance in their car. You should hear them tell about it. It was quite a ride for them. I knew little about it.

Once I was in the heart center, someone said to me, "We are going to move you over to the table now." Then I was gone. I was no longer conscious of the natural world.

Next, the surgeons ran into a major problem. They had given me an anesthetic that had had an adverse effect on me. It so happened that I was an exceptional individual who was sensitive to those particular chemicals. Given the nature and urgency of the surgery, there was no way for anyone to have known that I would have any kind of reaction to the anesthetic. I am thankful I had doctors who were proficient in their fields of expertise. They kept me alive during the surgery.

I was told that the team of doctors worked on me for about an hour before they could start the actual surgery.

The doctor who was the head of my surgical team said that everything had gone well. The surgery itself was a success.

It was during recovery that I ran into other critical situations. It is common practice to superdose heart-surgery patients with magnesium to aid the healing of the heart. But it turned out that I was one of those rare individuals who reacted poorly to the magnesium. This medication caused a lot of serious problems for me. For example, it caused a part of my brain to swell. The staff had to get it out of my system as soon as they could. I found out later that it would have affected my memory if it hadn't been flushed from my system.

The medical team tried seven different anesthetics on me to bring me out of unconsciousness. I reacted to these poorly. Not one of them worked. The lead doctor said that my blood pressure bottomed out every time they discontinued the anesthetic. They had to slowly decrease the anesthetics over a seven-day period before I was able to regain consciousness and be taken off of those medicines completely. I had an excellent team of doctors. The Lord was helping us all.

It was during this time that I flatlined twice. And each time I flatlined, I found myself with the Lord.

In the blink of an eye, the snap of my fingers, less than a second, I was with the Lord. It was in an instant of time. We just stood there enjoying one another and talking with one another. And we had the most wonderful conversations.

I heard his voice in three different ways. Sometimes I could hear it clearly in my head. At other times, he spoke clearly to me. And then there were times when he knew my thoughts and answered me before I would even ask him a question.

Jesus and I were standing in the air but not on a cloud. He did not take hold of my hand or my arm to hold me up. I did not go down a tunnel, following a bright light. The reason I share this information is because many times I've been asked whether or not I experienced things typical of a near-death experience.

Jesus had me look to my left. I had been so captivated by Jesus that my eyes were on him. We were standing there together and looking down upon a very spacious area of a sandy beach. The beach was wide, stretching as far as the eye could see. I was hearing waves roll in on the shore, but I could not see any water.

I felt a peace surrounding me as I listened to the lapping of the gentle waves on the shore. Peace and contentment overwhelmed me. I spent a long period of time just watching the beautiful beach as Jesus and I talked. I would think to myself, *I want to ask Jesus this.* Before I could ask him, he would answer me with a verse of Scripture, which he placed in my mind. Sometimes he would talk to me aloud, bringing things about the beach to my attention.

The Lord said to me that I had asked many times over a period of time, "How was it that people could love you so fervently one day and then crucify you the next?" Jesus spoke aloud to me, "A lot of things you have been experiencing these last few months have been a very small part of what I suffered. You will understand."

The peace and love that was all around me flooded my very being. I was so in awe of Jesus that I never said a word. I was so content to be with the Lord that my mind was on nothing else. Jesus and I spent a long period of time just watching the beautiful beach of light grayish and white sand. Time was not as we on earth know it to be. It seemed I was with Jesus for an hour, but it was only for a few seconds of time on earth.

The Lord drew my attention to the only person on the beach. I had noticed no one there before. The person, who never moved, was kneeling on the beach right below us. I watched very intently for a long time. All of a sudden, I realized that the praying person on the beach was me. I was hovering in the air with the Lord and looking down on myself. How could this be? My spirit was standing with the Lord, but on the beach was my body, which was nothing but a shell.

In a split second, I was on the beach with the Lord. The two of us were standing right next to my body. Then the Lord allowed my spirit to go back into my body. I watched as this happened. Back in my body on the sand, I was still on my knees praying.

The Lord's voice said, "Look at the sand." He then told me to pick up a handful. After doing as he asked, I looked at each grain and marveled at how alike they all were. They were very small and all had the same beautiful color. The Lord then told me to allow the sand to return to the beach. I allowed the sand to sift through my fingers and fall back to the beach, where it all ran together. The sand never could be arranged like it just had been and never could be separated in that same way again.

The Lord's thoughts were very clear in my mind. He informed me that each grain of sand represented a person. Billions and billions more grains of sand represented the people of earth. Then there was silence. There seemed to be a lengthy space of time here. I cannot tell you how long I watched. I just enjoyed the presence of the Lord.

The next thing I knew, the Lord and I were back in the air and looking down on the sandy beach. My body was bent over in a praying position on the sand. We watched for a long time. I knew that the Lord was going to send me back to earth. I said, "Jesus, please do not send me back. I do not want to go back."

Then the Lord said in the most kind and loving voice, "No, you must return. *I am with you.*" He then put a clear thought into my mind: *I have more for you to do.* I knew that he had reasons for sending me back.

I left in the same way that I had been brought to him. I was gone, away from his presence, in an instant. I was still not conscious and was not aware of anything going on in the waking world.

The Second Time I Was with the Lord

In an instant of time, I was back with the Lord Jesus, standing with him in the air. He had called me back. I was so glad to be with him again. His blessed peace and wonderful contentment flooded my very being. His love overwhelmed me. I was feeling a great agape sort of love. We spent a long time just watching the beautiful beach of light gray and white sand again. Time meant nothing to me.

This time, the Lord had me look to my right. He drew my attention to my body, which was again kneeling in prayer on the beach. Within a second of time, the Lord and I were back on the beach. He put my spirit back into my body again. I opened my eyes to see that the grains of sand had turned into golden nuggets of all sizes. The sun shone so brightly on the gold nuggets that there was a bright glare making it impossible for me to see the whole beach. The nuggets ranged in size. Some were as small as a green pea, and a few were as big as a double egg. The Lord had me pick up a few nuggets and hold them in my hand. Some were round; others were oblong or egg-shaped. Each one was smooth, glistening and sparkling in the beautiful light. It was the most spectacular sight I have ever seen. The brilliance of the light and the beauty of the light reflecting off the gold nuggets was breathtaking.

The golden nuggets were fewer in number than the grains of sand that on the previous beach represented everyone on earth. On this beach, each golden nugget represented a saint. The Lord very quickly said, "Every one of them has come through the fire. All of their impurities are gone."

Jesus then said, "Out of the multitudes of people represented by the sand, the golden nuggets represent, in comparison, the few who find me."

In my mind were these sentences: *Work. The time is short.* The communication between me and Jesus was telepathic at this time. He knew all of my thoughts, and I could hear his voice as clear in my mind as if he were speaking aloud. The Lord was showing me the purpose of work. He was also teaching me what happens when one really goes to work for him.

I was now back in the air with the Lord, very happy to be with him. We were looking down at the beach of golden nuggets once again. My body was bent over, praying on the beach. Jesus and I watched for a long time. My body never moved. My spirit was with the Lord.

Again I knew that Jesus was going to send me back to earth. I said again, "Please do not send me back. I want to stay with you."

The Lord replied, in the most kind and compassionate voice, "No! You must go back. You must return. *I am with you.*" Again in my mind, I knew he had something for me to do. He wanted more golden nuggets.

Jesus answered many questions that had been on my mind. The answers were just there. Then, the Lord sent me back to earth again.

The first thing I knew in the natural world was a nurse patting me on the face and calling my name rather loudly. I opened my eyes. She then said to me, "Do you know your name?"

I answered, "Betty."

She started yelling, saying, "We got her back."

She did not know what I was thinking. *You dummy. You are the nurse here and you don't know my name. I am the patient.* She then told me I was not at the heart center anymore. I had been moved to another hospital.

Now that was news to me. I learned later from a doctor that I had flatlined two times after surgery. It was then that I knew I had been with the Lord both of those times.

A few days later while I was recovering at home and was able to get up myself, my son Bob was sitting in the living room with me. He said, "Mom, I have waited a while to tell you this, but I feel now is the right time. I was praying for you the whole time you were in surgery. The Lord spoke to me and told me he was sending you back because he had something for you to do." I knew then that everything was going to be all right. God confirmed it through Bob that something had happened. Bob did not know what.

Bob said, "While I was in the chapel praying all the while you were in surgery, the Lord spoke to me. I was all alone in the chapel. A very firm voice said, 'Bob.' I looked all around. No one was there. I was all alone. Then the voice said, 'Bob, I am sending your mother back. I have something more for her to do.'"

God was showing me that he wants his followers to get busy and win more souls for his kingdom—and also that he had something for me to do. Many times God has dropped clear thoughts into my mind. The thoughts are either for me personally or for the body of Christ.

Attacked in the Middle of the Night

Wednesday, July 5, 2006

I was wakened about 3:30 a.m., the middle of the night. There was movement in the opposite corner of the bedroom. I had a small night-light on at the foot of the bed. There was a wavy, swaying motion in the far corner. It was as though a large transparent figure was there, moving very slowly from side to side. At the same time, it seemed to be moving slowly forward toward the end of the bed.

I spoke in a strong voice of command, "You evil of Satan, I bind you in the name of Jesus." The figure stopped and did not come any closer. I knew it was evil. I then spoke to it again. "You evil of Satan, in the name of Jesus I loose you to go back to the pit where you came from. Go back to where you came from in the name of Jesus. I thank you, Jesus." The figure slowly disappeared until it was entirely gone.

I kept thanking the Lord for what he had done for me. Satan does not like it when we praise the name of Jesus.

Attacked in the Middle of the Night 2

Friday, July 7, 2006

It was very hot that evening. I had left my bedroom window open. I was wakened around 3:00 a.m. by a feeling of heaviness that seemed to be drifting in through the window. It was slowly enveloping my lower legs, which felt a shivering sensation. The feeling was slowly coming up my legs. I knew I was being attacked again.

I said in a strong, loud voice, "Satan, I bind you in the name of Jesus." I knew I had to stop this sensation. It was going to kill me. Jesus stopped it. Then I commanded again, "You evil of Satan, I command you in the name of Jesus, go back to where you came from." I felt the pressure or grip that was around my legs release instantly. The presence slowly drifted back out of the window, which initially it had come through.

Jesus was preparing me to do battle when it was needed. The pastor at my church told me and the rest of the congregation that we needed to know about spiritual warfare. If we came up against it and had no knowledge of what to do, we would lose the battle.

We should put on our armor of God, he had said. We also had to know how to use it. It was for our protection.

You need to take one piece of the armor and study it. Go on to the next piece when you understand the previous one. Every Christian needs to know how to put on the armor of God, what it is for, and how to use it.

> Put on the whole armor of God, that ye may be able to stand against the wiles of the devil.

> For we wrestle not against flesh and blood, but against principalities, against powers, against the rulers of the darkness of this world, against spiritual wickedness in high places.

> Wherefore take unto you the whole armor of God, that ye may be able to withstand in the evil day, and having done all, to stand.

> Stand therefore, having your loins girt about with truth, and having on the breastplate of righteousness.

> And your feet shod with the preparation of the gospel of peace;

> Above all, taking the shield of faith, wherewith ye shall be able to quench all the fiery darts of the wicked.

> And take the helmet of salvation, and the sword of the Spirit, which is the word of God:

Praying always with all prayer and supplication in the Spirit, and watching thereunto with all perseverance and supplication for all saints.

Ephesians 6:11–18

Learn to put on the armor of God daily. You never know when you will need it.

Small Country Church
with White Paint

Thursday, March 29, 2007

In this dream, I was sitting in the back of the church watching the congregation of people clapping, singing, and worshipping the Lord. At first the singing seemed happy and joyful. At first I seemed to be joyful as I watched everyone in this packed little church. But an empty feeling came over me the longer I sat there watching. I was watching the smiling, joyful faces of people who were clapping and swaying to the music. Something was happening to them. With all this going on, there was an emptiness that seemed to be coming over their faces.

I knew what the problem was. I slowly got out of my seat at the back of the church and walked down the middle aisle, moving toward the front. The people were all still laughing and singing, but the joy of the Lord was not with them. I turned, walked to my right, and crossed in front of the people in the front row. I made my way to a set of steps that angled back and led up onto the altar.

114

Everyone had been singing joyfully, but there was something missing. I walked slowly across to the middle of the altar and turned toward the crowd. I raised both hands into the air and just stood there. A hush came upon the crowd. There was a silence that seemed to last a long while.

I softly started to sing, "Holy Spirit, thou art welcome in this place." Softly the people started singing. Their arms went up and their faces turned upward. Over and over we sang, "Holy Spirit, thou art welcome in this place." The Holy Spirit filled the room. Every person was feeling the presence of the Comforter. I do not know how long this went on. It seemed that the beautiful presence of the Holy Spirit was there for a very long time.

I suddenly found myself outside, behind the church, and alone. Everyone had gone home. All the lights were out except for one at the front of the church. I wanted to go back inside but did not know why. The back door to the church was open, and it seemed that there was no one inside. All of a sudden a little toddler who was just learning to walk was coming toward the door. I did not want to touch the child. The mother did not know that I was there. I just stood in front of the door to block her from coming out. I started to call out to the mother, but she called out to the child, saying it was time to go. The child turned around and was heading back to the front of the church toward her mother. I never saw the mother; I just knew that she was there.

The thing that stood out to me was that all the joyful singing was dead without the Holy Spirit. The group in the church had not had any teaching about the Holy Spirit, as most of them were new Christians. The mother in the dream represented the church. She needed to teach the children. The little child represented all of the new Christians who needed to be taught so they would not wander out into the dark and get lost.

The world is a scary place without Jesus. The Holy Spirit is here to teach us and help us.

False Doctrine

Saturday, April 11, 2007—A Vision

Someone was fighting a spider. It was a huge one, about sixteen inches long. The person, who was outside trying to prevent the spider from coming into the building, couldn't seem to kill it.

I had no idea where I was. I was standing just inside the open door of a large wooden building. Then the spider turned on me. It was going to jump. I grabbed a board from just inside the door. When the spider jumped, I hit it hard with the board, but this only made it run off.

A little bit later the spider returned.

The second time I encountered the spider, I hit it again. This time it had run under a huge beautiful tree with large green leaves. It lay on the ground and turned in circles. The spider was stunned, not knowing what to do.

It took another big lunge at me. I had a large book in my hands. As the spider jumped at me, I took a swing at it with the book and smacked it hard. The spider cracked, as if I had hit a big hard rock or something else solid. I then realized that the book I was holding in my hands was a Bible. I had hit the spider with the Bible and it had gone flying backwards through the air to alight on a rocky (or torn-up blacktop) road. I walked over and stood above the spider. My first thought was that it was dead.

I turned and started to walk away into a yard of nice green grass. Something in my mind was telling me to go back and check on the spider to make sure it was dead. I turned around, walked back, and stood over the creature. I had seen spiders flatten out like this one in order to play dead. With great determination to make sure this thing was dead, I stomped on it as hard as I could. It was dead. It was lying there in pieces that were sprawled out over the ground. I had smashed it.

After seeing that I had smashed the spider, I started to walk back across the yard. This was the end of the vision.

The Meaning of the Vision

The first thing the Lord wanted to show me with this vision was that the spider stood for false doctrine.

Someone I did not know was trying to fight this spider (false doctrine). This individual was trying to keep it from coming into the building. Then the spider, false doctrine, was trying to get past me in order to enter the building. There was a board lying on the floor beside me. I picked it up and used it to hit the spider (false doctrine) hard. I knocked the spider outdoors into the grass.

From now on I will refer to the spider as false doctrine.

The false doctrine took a different direction to get inside the building. The second time I hit the false doctrine, it was confused about what to do. It then crawled under a sturdy tree that was everlasting and had great strength. This tree represented God's great eternal power. The false doctrine was turning in circles and didn't know which way to go. It could not stand being under this tree. The Word of God was confusing it. God was letting me know that his Word is sharper than a two-edged sword.

Then false doctrine turned on me and lunged at me. I hit it hard with a large book I suddenly found in my hands. This was the Bible, the Word of God, which would defeat false doctrine. The false doctrine went sailing through the air and landed on a rough blacktop road. I walked over and stood over the false doctrine. I thought it was dead.

I walked away into a yard of beautiful soft green grass. I was beginning to feel rest and peace. Then my mind started thinking I should go back and check on this false doctrine. I walked back and stood over the false doctrine. It was flattened out and playing dead. I stomped on it. Now it was dead for sure.

I was walking through the beautiful soft green grass again. This time I was filled with peace and contentment to know that the false doctrine could be driven out with the Word of God. This was the end of the vision.

Christians are going to need to recognize false doctrine. Christians need to study the Bible. Christians need to pray. Christians need to get into a good Bible-study class. Christians need to develop friendships with other Bible-based Christians. Christians need to stop doing things and going to places that are harmful to their Christian walk.

An Angel Protecting Me

November 2, 2007

It was around the time when I generally get up in the morning, 6:00. At first I had a little sleep left in my eyes, but then my eyes were wide open. Suddenly I was looking through my bedroom wall, down through the kitchen, and out the window that was above the sink. I was watching a young man in his twenties sitting outside the window. He had his feet pulled up and his arms wrapped around his legs. He was leaning back against the yellow brick just outside of the window. He had a short haircut and was wearing a light green pullover sweater with jeans, looking very well dressed. I was very impressed that he looked perfect.

I was shocked all of a sudden. What was he sitting on? There was a hedge running from the front entrance and across the front of the house to the garage door. It sat a good ten to twelve inches from the house. The young man was sitting on thin air. It was like he was sitting on something solid, but nothing was there. Even if the hedge had been near the house, it could not have held his weight. He would have sunk down into the branches.

The young man's feet were resting on something solid that was not there. He looked very comfortable and relaxed. He would turn his head one way and look for a while; next he would look all around; and then he would look the other way. It was as if he was looking for someone.

In my mind I heard, as clear as could be, "You asked me to send an angel to protect you and your home." Once I heard this, my mind returned to what I had prayed for the night before. I had been a little uneasy about something and had asked the Lord for his protection. He not only gave me that protection but also allowed me to see the angel that had been protecting me. God is very good.

New World Religion

January 7, 2009

I listen to reruns of Lester Sumrall's teachings on TV every morning while preparing my breakfast. On this particular day, he was talking about how Christians had trials and tribulations and how Christians would be persecuted during the end times. When it came time for a station break, I wanted to hear the weather report. I had switched channels and was now listening to two men talking. I started to switch channels again, but one of the men said that he was going to discuss a new religion. A scroll ran on the screen that had every Christian denomination and religion listed on it. It was a long list. I sat down on the couch and wanted to hear about this new religion. The men said that this religion incorporated all religions. They talked about another religion and said that it was now greater than Christianity in the United States. The followers of this religion had men placed all over the United States to build churches in every state. One of the men then very pointedly said, "The people who are Christians will have to learn to get along with them, because this is the new world religion."

In this new church, everyone would worship their own God. Hearing that almost shocked me out of my seat. After that statement was made, the broadcast ended. The last words I had heard were, "This is the new world religion."

God had everything worked out in order to make the dream I'd had about false doctrine clear to me. He was preparing me for it. God was telling me not to get caught up in false doctrine. He was telling me that many Christians will accept this new world religion because they can practice it and still worship God.

True Christians have a close walk with God. There are some who have been pretending to be Christians for a long time without ever accepting Jesus as Lord and Savior of their life. Every one of us should be developing a closer walk with the Lord. No one is exempt. False doctrine will slowly capture the person who does not have a close walk with the Lord.

God tells us in Matthew 24:5, "For many shall come in my name, saying, 'I am Christ,' and shall deceive many."

Matthew 24:24 reads, "For there shall arise false Christ, and false prophets, and shall show great signs and wonders; insomuch that, if it were possible, they shall deceive the very elect."

You may be interested in reading a book written by my son Robert. *Three Prayers* reveals the three most critical prayers that every Christian should be praying in these last days.

Three Prayers by Robert North is a must for those who desire to protect themselves in this present day and to prepare themselves for the future.